CHALLENGING

MOSCOW'S

MESSAGE

AFPC

Library of Congress Control Number: 2023946086

Paperback - 978-1-956450-89-7
Ebook - 978-1-956450-90-3

**AMERICAN FOREIGN
POLICY COUNCIL**

AFPC Press
American Foreign Policy Council
509 C Street NE
Washington, DC 20002

in association with

ARMINLEAR

Armin Lear Press Inc
215 W Riverside Drive, #4362
Estes Park, CO 80517

CONTENTS

CHALLENGING

MOSCOW'S

MESSAGE

Russian Disinformation and the Western Response

ILAN BERMAN

AFPC

ACKNOWLEDGMENTS

First and foremost, special thanks go to my friend and colleague Monika Richter, who has helped tremendously in shaping my understanding of the contemporary threat posed by Russian disinformation. Monika has likewise been indispensable in assisting me in grasping the benefits – and the limits – of the Western response to it so far.

I gleaned enormous insights into Russian strategy, and the role disinformation plays in it, from experts like Stephen Blank, Don Jensen, Brian Whitmore, Natalya Arno, Peter Doran, Mollie Saltskog, Ivana Stradner and Joseph Humire. At the same time, a host of former government officials, including Elizabeth Robbins, David Wilezol and Alberto Fernandez, as well as a range of specialists currently serving at the U.S. Agency for Global Media, in the U.S. Congress, and at the Department of State, helped me better understand the scope of the U.S. government's contemporary public diplomacy, messaging and counter-disinformation efforts.

Much of the first-hand research for this study was carried out between October 2022 and February 2023, and entailed visits to Belgium, the Czech Republic, Estonia, Latvia, Lithuania and Sweden. During those trips, I benefited from extensive conversations with numerous experts, scholars and officials on the frontlines of the fight against Russian disinformation. Their insights and experiences gave me a front row seat to Europe's evolving counter-disinformation scene – as well as so me (hopefully useful) ideas about how to improve it.

Finally, this project benefitted from the assistance of diligent researchers at the American Foreign Policy Council, including Marian Searby and Dinah Gorayeb, who helped fill in blanks in my research and update my case studies. And there are, of course, many others who helped with this work who must by necessity remain nameless. They all have my gratitude and heartfelt thanks. My hope is that I have managed to synthesize their thoughts and ideas into a study that advances the Western understanding of how Russia manipulates the information sphere, and what is needed to successfully fight against it.

ILAN BERMAN
Washington, DC
August 2023

THE LONG ARC
OF RUSSIAN
DISINFORMATION

The phenomenon of disinformation is far from new. While the term is now distorted by overuse, as well as by its conflation with ideas such as "fake news" that permeate contemporary politics, it is a concept with both a long history and a distinct strategic purpose – one that represents among the most enduring and well-established tools of Soviet (and now Russian) asymmetric warfare.

To be sure, the use of propaganda and deception in politics and war has a long history, dating back millennia. Even so, the Russian relationship with – and weaponization of – disinformation as a tool of statecraft stands out, both for its effectiveness and for its durability. Quite simply, information manipulation has long served as a seminal shaping tool in the Kremlin's interactions with the world. And today, because of a changed global media environment and the increasingly adversarial, expansionist foreign policy being pursued by Russia under Vladimir Putin, it has arguably assumed greater significance than ever before.

THE LOGIC OF DISINFORMATION

Why has Moscow relied so heavily over the years on the use and manipulation of information? The answer can be found in the way the Kremlin thinks about both politics and policy. This thinking has proven to be remarkably durable for more than a century and has informed the approaches of successive Soviet leaders (and subsequently those of Russia) to their country's relationship and ideological competition with the West.

At its core is the notion that – in stark contrast with the way Western leaders view them – war and peace are not in fact fundamentally different concepts. As the scholars Richard Schultz and Roy Godson succinctly explained in their Cold War study of the subject, "Soviet leaders do not regard war and politics as distinct conditions; rather, from their perspective, politics is a continual state of war carried on by a wide variety of means."[1] And while military operations doubtless represented one of those methods, they were far from the most desirable, both because of the human costs associated with overt conflict and because of the chronic resource constraints suffered by the USSR, which placed Moscow at a disadvantage in many conventional force-on-force scenarios and bred a penchant for "unconventional warfare" on the part of the Kremlin.[2]

As a result, beginning in the 1950s, the Soviet Union placed significant emphasis on the development of techniques for influencing foreign behavior short of war. This field, broadly known as "active measures" (*aktivniye meropriyatiya* in Russian), quickly became the Kremlin's main strategy to shape events and policy in other countries.[3] It was this activity, rather than traditional espionage, which occupied the lion's share of attention and

1   Richard H. Shultz and Roy Godson, *Dezinformatsiya: Active Measures in Soviet Strategy* (Pergamon-Brassey's, 1984), 1-2.

2   See, for instance, Patrick J. Savage, "The Conventionality of Russia's Unconventional Warfare," *Parameters* 48, no. 2 (2018), https://press.armywarcollege.edu/cgi/viewcontent.cgi?article=2946&context=parameters.

3   Hon. C.W. Bill Young, "Soviet Active Measures in the United States – An Updated Report by the FBI," *Congressional Record* E 4716, December 9, 1987, https://www.cia.gov/readingroom/docs/CIA-RDP11M01338R000400470089-2.pdf.

resources on the part of the KGB, the Soviet Union's main foreign intelligence agency, defectors have divulged.[4]

The objectives of Soviet "active measures" were extremely ambitious. As KGB defector Yuri Bezmenov explained in a now-famous 1985 television interview, they involved a "slow process... to change the perception of reality of every American to such an extent that, despite the abundance of information, no-one is able to come to sensible conclusions in the interests of defending themselves, their families, their community and their country."[5] "Active measures" encompassed a wide array of information manipulation tactics and psychological warfare, with disinformation prominent among them.

Disinformation, or *dezinformatsiya*, refers to a specific tactic developed by the early Soviet KGB (drawing from the earlier practices of the Tsarist-era secret police, known as the *Okhrana*[6]) to weaken adversaries through information manipulation. Soviet disinformation used mass media to insert

---

4   G. Edward Griffin, "Soviet Subversion of the Free-World Press: A Conversation with Yuri Bezmenov," 1985, https://www.youtube.com/watch?v=pOmXiapfCs8.

5   Ibid.

6   Marcel H. Van Herpen, *Putin's Propaganda Machine: Soft Power and Russian Foreign Policy* (Rowman & Littlefield, 2016), 3.

and circulate false information – either overtly or covertly – into enemy communications, with the intent of deceiving the target audience and shifting public opinion to Moscow's advantage. Soviet disinformation campaigns involved deliberate distortions propagated through a variety of techniques, "ranging from the most primitive, like rumors and forgeries, to the most sophisticated, such as secretly purchasing mass media abroad and using them as permanent channels of disinformation."[7] These methods, Schultz and Godson note, were used "to strengthen allies and weaken opponents and to create a favorable environment for the achievement of Soviet foreign policy objectives," and were "systematically and routinely conducted on a worldwide scale."[8]

In its development, disinformation derived from the longstanding Russian military tradition of *maskirovka*, or strategic deception, which encompasses a variety of "actions and conditions that fall short of war" but are designed to ensure victory

---

7 Ladislav Bittman, "The Use of Disinformation by Democracies," *International Journal of Intelligence and CounterIntelligence* 4, no. 2, 1990, 248.

8 Shultz and Godson, *Dezinformatsiya: Active Measures in Soviet Strategy*, 2.

before the first weapons are drawn.[9] Closely associated is the concept of "reflexive control," which theorizes that one can manipulate an opponent using deception techniques in order to compel them to make significant tactical and strategic errors against their own self-interest.[10] "Reflexive control" is a process of political warfare and subversion, conducted primarily in the information domain, that seeks to alter a target's behavior or decision-making to the advantage of the Kremlin's strategic objectives, and do so without the target even realizing it. In pursuit of this objective, the Soviet Union focused on aggressive deception operations aimed at weakening its adversaries throughout the duration of the Cold War.

COLD WAR APPLICATIONS

Beginning in the early 20th century, scholars of propaganda theorized that there were three distinct types: white, grey, and black. These modes were determined not by the content of the propaganda

9   JB Vowell, "Maskirovka: From Russia with Deception," *RealClearDefense*, October 31, 2016, https://www. realcleardefense.com/articles/2016/10/31/maskirovka_ from_russia_with_deception_110282.html

10   See, for instance, Nicholas Cull et al., *Soviet Subversion, Disinformation and Propaganda: How the West Fought Against It*, LSE Consulting, October 2017, https://www.lse. ac.uk/iga/assets/documents/arena/2018/Jigsaw-Soviet-Subversion-Disinformation-and-Propaganda-Final-Report.pdf

itself, but rather by the transparency of the sources it employed. While white propaganda relies on sources that are either openly identified or can be easily inferred, black propaganda derives from those deliberately set up to deceive. Grey propaganda, meanwhile, comes from sources that cannot be definitively attributed.

The Soviet Union pursued a hostile, primarily black-and-grey propaganda policy aimed at Western publics and designed to confuse and mislead its targets via psychological and information warfare. Grey outlets included Soviet-funded front organizations, while black propaganda involved explicit disinformation campaigns. This typically involved attempts to plant politically advantageous stories in the media sources of other countries, either without indicating the source of the information or with outright attribution to a legitimate source.[11] These stories capitalized upon existing fears and prejudices about the United States, either domestically within America itself, as a way of sowing internal divisions, or in other countries in order to undermine support for and alignment with the U.S. government.

---

11   Roy Godson and Richard Shultz, "Soviet Active Measures: Distinctions and Definitions," *Defense Analysis* 1, no. 2, 1985, 104.

The goals of this effort were sweeping in nature. In their comprehensive 1984 study of Soviet disinformation, Schultz and Godson identified six discrete objectives of the USSR's propaganda and political warfare:

1. To influence American, European, and world public opinion to believe that U.S. military and political policies are the major cause of international conflict and crisis.

2. To demonstrate that the United States is an aggressive, militaristic, and imperialistic power.

3. To isolate the United States from its friends and allies, especially those in the North Atlantic Treaty Organization (NATO), and to discredit those states that cooperate with the United States.

4. To discredit the U.S. and NATO military and intelligence establishments.

5. To demonstrate that the policies and objectives of the United States are incompatible with those of the underdeveloped nations.

6. To confuse world public opinion
   concerning Soviet global ambitions,
   creating a favorable environment for
   Soviet foreign policy.[12]

Western publics were thus considered not just legitimate but indispensable targets of Soviet deception and psychological warfare. And from the start, in keeping with the Soviet conception of the United States as the *glavnie vrag* (main adversary), a significant portion of the USSR's disinformation activities were aimed at America and the American people.

In support of these objectives, the USSR erected an elaborate bureaucracy of influence. Overseen by the Politburo and Secretariat of the Communist Party of the Soviet Union (CPSU), it entailed multiple branches, each dealing with a different aspect of the disinformation and propaganda mission. The CPSU's International Information Department oversaw official messaging organs like the TASS and Novosti news agencies, the production of books, and the dissemination of newspapers like *Pravda*. The International Department of the CPSU oversaw contacts with foreign

---

12   Shultz and Godson, *Dezinformatsiya: Active Measures in Soviet Strategy*, 40.

communist parties, revolutionary movements, and "national front organizations" that advanced Moscow's messaging and objectives abroad. And the First Chief Directorate of the KGB, the USSR's premier spy agency, was put in charge of "covert propaganda" and disinformation.[13] The function of this last line of effort was "to reinforce themes promoted through Soviet outlets of overt propaganda," including through the "clandestine placement" of media items in foreign news outlets and the selective amplification of previously published foreign articles for geopolitical advantage.[14]

Among the most effective efforts in this regard was a campaign known as OPERATION: INFEKTION. In October 1985, the Soviet journal *Literaturnaya Gazeta* published an article, sourced from earlier coverage in an Indian newspaper that had been covertly set up by the KGB in the 1960s, claiming that the HIV/AIDS virus had been created by the U.S. government as part of a biological weapons research program. The fabricated story was then picked up by other agents of Soviet propaganda and disseminated further, to great effect. Within two years, the disinformation

---

13   Detailed in Shultz and Godson, *Dezinformatsiya*, 20.

14   Ibid., 32.

campaign had been reported in more than eighty different countries and thirty languages.[15] The narrative proved effective because it deftly played on the political climate of the times. Earlier revelations of CIA chemical and biological weapons research had instilled a culture of distrust among ordinary Americans, while panic surrounding the AIDS epidemic, which was then poorly understood even by the scientific community, helped fuel speculation about the origins of the virus.[16] The Soviet campaign was designed to exploit these organic dynamics to discredit the U.S. government, as well as to distract from accusations about the USSR's own experimentation with biological weapons.[17]

The story drew outrage from the U.S. government, which subsequently made extensive efforts to debunk the false narrative. So, too, did the international scientific community, which warned that the scientific field was being used for political and propaganda purposes. Yet the INFEKTION story proved resilient; it was not until 1987 that the Soviet leadership, under tremendous pressure from both the United States and scientific quarters,

15 Thomas Boghardt, "Soviet Bloc Intelligence and Its AIDS Disinformation Campaign," *Studies in Intelligence* 53, no. 4, December 2009, 7.

16 Ibid., 4.

17 Ibidem.

officially disowned it.[18] However, the effects were tremendously far-reaching. A 2005 study in the medical journal *The Lancet* found that, some three decades after the launch of INFEKTION, one in three African Americans still believed HIV was produced in a government lab, and one in seven was convinced the disease had been created by the US government to control the country's Black population.[19]

THE SOVIET COLLAPSE, AND AFTER

The dissolution of the USSR in 1991 wrought massive changes to the structure of power that had prevailed in the country for the preceding seven decades, and to its place in the world.

During the early 1990s, the power of the KGB diminished, as the once all-powerful Soviet intelligence agency (first rebranded the FSK, and subsequently as the FSB) was broken up into constituent parts during the tenure of President Boris Yeltsin. For a brief period, real reform seemed possible, as true champions of change – like Russian

---

18 Christopher Andrew and Vasili Mitrokhin, *The World Was Going Our Way: The KGB and the Battle for the Third World: Newly Revealed Secrets from the Mitrokhin Archive* (New York: Basic Books, 2005), 621.

19 Editorial, "Conspiracy theories of HIV/AIDS," *The Lancet* 365, iss. 9458, February 2005, https://www.sciencedirect.com/science/article/abs/pii/S0140673605178751?via%3Dihub.

politician Vadim Bakatin – launched a valiant effort to dismantle the sprawling bureaucracy of intrigue, terror and unaccountable power that had been wielded by the Soviet secret police.[20]

This effort ultimately proved futile, however. By the mid-1990s, a process of reconsolidation had begun, as the FSB regained power and authority over vital government functions. The result was a reconstituted, revitalized intelligence bureaucracy – albeit one with more autonomy, and without the party and political control that had prevailed during the Soviet era. And with the rise of Vladimir Putin, a former KGB official, to the Russian presidency in the last days of 1999, the agency once again assumed a central place as an organ of state power in the new Russia.[21]

Russian disinformation charted a similar trajectory. The breakup of the Soviet Union in 1991, followed by the chaos of Russia's short-lived experiment with democratization in the 1990s, offered at least a brief reprieve from the Kremlin's use of deception and subversion against its adversaries,

---

20 For a detailed examination of this effort, see J. Michael Waller, *Secret Empire: The KGB in Russia Today* (Westview Press, 1994).

21 See generally Andrei Soldatov and Irina Borogan, *The New Nobility: The Restoration of Russia's Security State and the Enduring Legacy of the KGB* (PublicAffairs, 2011).

most directly the United States and NATO. This shift was buttressed by a qualitatively different worldview held by a handful of Russian officials who believed in the potential for a cooperative relationship between Moscow and Washington.[22] This outlook, however, waned in influence in parallel with the resurgence of the KGB. And as the Soviet era secret police ascended to prominence anew, so too did one of its most tried-and-true tactics. Under Putin, Russia resurrected disinformation as a core part of its international intelligence operations, and presciently adapted it to exploit the modern informational environment.

DISINFORMATION UNDER THE PUTIN REGIME

Indeed, in Putin's Russia, propaganda and information warfare have become critical elements of state policy and national security strategy. Thus, less than a year after Putin assumed the Russian presidency, the Kremlin issued a foreign policy and information doctrine laying out that the country faces an array of threats in the information domain, including the "information influence of foreign

---

22 For a detailed accounting of this period, see Andrei *Kozyrev, The Firebird: The Elusive Fate of Russian Democracy* (University of Pittsburgh Press, 2020).

political, economic, military and information structures on [...] Russian foreign policy strategy," as well as the "propaganda activities of political forces, nongovernmental associations, mass media and individuals." These activities, it argued, "distort" the "foreign policy activities of the Russian Federation."[23] To counter them, the doctrine advocated "stepping up counter-propaganda activities aimed at preventing the negative consequences of the dissemination of disinformation about the internal policy of Russia" and "neutraliz[ing] the disinformation being disseminated [abroad] on the foreign policy of the Russian Federation."[24]

These priorities have proved enduring. A decade later, the country's 2010 defense doctrine formally authorized the use of information warfare to proactively shape the global order, and to condition the international environment to Russia's subsequent use of military force.[25] Three years after that, Russia's top uniformed military official, Chief of Staff of the Armed Forces General Valery Gerasimov, articulated a series of guiding

---

23 Russian Federation, *Information Security Doctrine of the Russian Federation*, 2000, https://base.garant.ru/182535.

24 Ibid.

25 The Kremlin, "Military Doctrine of the Russian Federation," February 5, 2010. An English language translation is available at https://carnegieendowment.org/files/2010russia_military_doctrine.pdf.

principles for modern warfare in the Russian newspaper *Voyenno-Promyshlennyy Kurier*. These principles, which have come to be thought of in the West, erroneously[26], as the "Gerasimov Doctrine," include the idea that information dominance was essential to military victory in an era of increasingly asymmetric conflict.[27] Indeed, the 2021 *National Security Strategy of the Russian Federation* identifies "information security" as a core area of concern, and emphasizes the importance of the "development of forces and means of information confrontation" as a national security priority.[28]

In support of these objectives, the Kremlin has dedicated enormous resources toward the creation

---

26 As numerous scholars have noted, Gerasimov himself was not the architect of Russia's contemporary information security doctrine. His contribution was simply to aggregate the enumerated principles in one place.

27 "[T]he informational space opens wide asymmetrical possibilities for reducing the fighting potential of the enemy," Gerasimov argues. As a result, "[i]t is necessary to perfect activities in the information space, including the defense of our own objectives." Valery Gerasimov, "The Value of Science Is in the Foresight," *Voyenno-Promyshlennyy Kurier,* February 27, 2013, https://vpk-news.ru/articles/14632. An English translation of the article is available in the January-February 2016 edition of the journal *Military Review*. It can be found online at https://www.armyupress.army.mil/portals/7/military-review/archives/english/militaryreview_20160228_art008.pdf.

28 President of the Russian Federation, *Strategia Natsionalnoye Bezopastnostii Rosiyskoy Federatstii* [National Security Strategy of the Russian Federation], July 2, 2021, http://actual.pravo.gov.ru/text.html#pnum=0001202107030001.

of outlets, agencies and mechanisms by which to disseminate Moscow's view of the world – and denigrate Western ideas, values and societies, including:

- The establishment, in 2005, of a dedicated 24-hour media channel, known as *Russia Today* (more recently, simply *RT*), to serve as a competitor to Western media outlets such as *CNN*, the *BBC* and others, and to promote Russia's worldview to foreign audiences.[29] As of 2016, *RT* was estimated to command a budget of more than $300 million annually.[30]

- The subsequent creation, in 2014, of the state-owned *Sputnik* news agency as a supplemental means of external messaging. It is designed to broadcast in some 30 different languages (including all of the languages of the former Soviet

---

29 Van Herpen, *Putin's Propaganda Machine: Soft Power and Russian Foreign Policy*, 67-93.

30 Christopher Paul and Miriam Mathews, "The Russian 'Firehose of Falsehood' Propaganda Model: Why It Might Work and Options to Counter It," *RAND Corporation Perspective* no. 198, 2016, https://www.rand.org/pubs/perspectives/PE198.html.

Union) and produce more than 800 hours of radio programming daily.[31]

- A constellation of other outlets (print, broadcast and digital), such as RUPTLY and Maffick, that serve to augment the messaging and reach of Russia's main propaganda organs.[32]

- The acquisition of stakes in assorted Western newspapers via Kremlin-aligned oligarchs, and their subsequent manipulation of news content and coverage.[33]

- Expanding control over the domestic social media sphere within Russia, via censorship and onerous laws restricting free speech as well as the establishment

31 See Antonio Missiroli et al., "Strategic Communications from the East," in *Strategic Communications: East and South* (European Union Institute for Security Studies, 2016), https://www.jstor.org/stable/resrep07092.5?seq=1. See also Matthew Hilburn, "Russia's New World Broadcast Service is 'Sputnik,'" Voice of America, November 10, 2014, https://www.voanews.com/a/russia-launches-new-media-brand-called-sputnik/2515216.html.

32 U.S. Department of State, Global Engagement Center, *Kremlin-Funded Media: RT and Sputnik's Role in Russia's Disinformation and Propaganda Ecosystem,* January 2022, https://www.state.gov/wp-content/uploads/2022/01/Kremlin-Funded-Media_January_update-19.pdf.

33 Van Herpen, *Putin's Propaganda Machine: Soft Power and Russian Foreign Policy,* 67-93.

of domestic platforms, like *vKontakte*, to compete with Western analogues.[34]

- The formation of a cadre of dedicated patriotic bloggers – a veritable "troll army" – that could incrementally (via comments, posts and other activities) shift discourse relating to Russia in both domestic and international media.[35]

- The empowerment of proxy agencies, like the notorious Internet Research Agency (IRA) troll farm of oligarch Yevgeny Prigozhin, to carry out private sector but Kremlin-aligned information warfare on Western societies.[36] (At the height of its effectiveness, the IRA was an essential component of Russia's disinformation ecosystem, with an estimated 400 staffers working 12-hour shifts, and eighty employees dedicated specifically to operations designed to disrupt the U.S. political system.) Researchers have gauged that the content generated by

---

34 Ibid.

35 Paul and Mathews, "The Russian 'Firehose of Falsehood' Propaganda Model."

36 Adrian Chen, "The Agency," *New York Times*, June 2, 2015, https://www.nytimes.com/2015/06/07/magazine/the-agency.html.

these "troll farms" reaches some 140 million internet users monthly just in the United States.[37]

The end result is an elaborate web of overlapping agencies, initiatives and lines of effort that the Kremlin has erected to advance its foreign policy and national security priorities. In its 2020 report on Russian disinformation, the State Department's Global Engagement Center (GEC) described this "ecosystem" as a "collection of official, proxy, and unattributed communication channels and platforms that Russia uses to create and amplify false narratives." "The ecosystem," it continued, "consists of five main pillars: official government communications, state-funded global messaging, cultivation of proxy sources, weaponization of social media, and cyber-enabled disinformation. The Kremlin bears direct responsibility for cultivating these tactics and platforms as part of its approach to using information as a weapon."[38] Scholars have likened the cumulative output of these outlets to a

37   See, for instance, David Kirichenko, "Thanks to AI, the Wagner mutiny will only briefly hamper Russian disinformation," *The Hill*, July 11, 2023, https://thehill.com/opinion/technology/4084125-thanks-to-ai-the-wagner-mutiny-will-only-briefly-hamper-russian-disinformation/.

38   U.S. Department of State, Global Engagement Center, *GEC Special Report: Pillars of Russia's Disinformation and Propaganda Ecosystem*, August 2020, https://www.state.gov/wp-content/uploads/2020/08/Pillars-of-Russia's-Disinformation-and-Propaganda-Ecosystem_08-04-20.pdf

"firehose of falsehood" which the Kremlin uses to obscure objective truth, outshout and out-maneuver legitimate news sources, and advance its own version of world events through "high-volume, multichannel, and continuous messaging."[39]

NEW MEDIA, NEW OPPORTUNITIES

This extensive architecture of influence has, in turn, been amplified by today's more crowded global media environment. In recent years, a growing deluge of news and opinion has changed the complexion of the global information sphere. Traditional sources of media are increasingly being challenged by new (and often unreliable) information outlets, while the proliferation of social media platforms has left users vulnerable to opaque algorithms and the biases of unaccountable editors. Simultaneously, the provision of information has undergone a "flattening," as once-authoritative sources are increasingly contested, and established knowledge is crowded out more and more by opinions that conform to the selective attitudes and biases of readers.[40]

Russian disinformation is thriving in this new

---

39 Paul and Miriam, "The Russian 'Firehose of Falsehood' Propaganda Model."

40 For a general discussion of the potential dangers of this shift, see Tom Nichols, *The Death of Expertise: The Campaign against Established Knowledge and Why It Matters* (Oxford University Press, 2017).

environment, with Kremlin-aligned disinformation actors deftly exploiting these changes to gain greater resonance for their messaging and to reach new audiences. To this end, recent years have seen the Kremlin make major investments in the expansion of its media outreach beyond its traditional ambit of the *Russkiy Mir* (Russian world) and Europe, into the developing world. Since the start of the Kremlin's current war against Ukraine in February 2022, in turn, the activities of this informational ecosystem have been scaled up significantly.

In Latin America, for instance, Russia is now operating a formidable media enterprise (consisting of multiple broadcast networks, social media messaging, and propaganda) that outstrips U.S. media engagement in the scope and breadth of its outreach toward regional states, experts say. Through it, Moscow has helped fuel regional grievances surrounding territory and politics, contributing to contemporary tensions in the region.[41] In Africa, meanwhile, Moscow's propaganda outlets have played upon local fears of economic hardship and food insecurity since the start of the war in

---

41   Interview with Joseph Michael Humire, AFPC
     Disinformation Wars podcast, episode 27, December
     22, 2022, https://podcasters.spotify.com/pod/show/
     afpcdisinfowarfare/episodes/EPISODE-27-Russian-
     disinformation-is-helping-reshape-Latin-America-e1sjilf/a-
     a937q9g.

Ukraine. As a summer 2022 analysis by the State Department's Global Engagement Center (GEC) noted, the Russian government and its proxies have been carrying out a "massive disinformation campaign" shifting the blame for rising global food and energy prices to the West in a campaign that is "intended to both hide Russia's culpability and persuade leaders of at-risk countries to support an end to sanctions designed to stop Russia's unjust and brutal war in Ukraine."[42] And in the Middle East, Russia is waging a "disinformation war" to shape regional opinion, amplifying false narratives and conspiracy theories via Arabic-language social media outlets and pushing its own propaganda via state-owned media channels, all of which boast Arab-language programming.[43]

This activity has had a material effect on global sentiment. While in the United States and Europe, opposition to Russia's war of aggression against Ukraine is widespread, Moscow is making major

42 U.S. Department of State, Global Engagement Center, "Russia's Disinformation Campaign Cannot Hide its Responsibility for the Global Food Crisis," June 22, 2022, https://www.state.gov/disarming-disinformation/russias-disinformation-cannot-hide-its-responsibility-for-the-global-food-crisis/.

43 See, for instance, H.A. Hellyer, "Russia is waging a disinformation war in the Middle East," *Politico Europe,* April 7, 2023, https://www.politico.eu/article/vladimir-putin-sputnik-rt-russia-is-waging-a-disinformation-war-in-the-middle-east/.

gains in advancing its position—and eroding that of the West – throughout the developing world, thanks to its propaganda and messaging capabilities. Thus, the 2023 edition of the Democracy Perception Index, the world's largest annual study on democracy, found a wide gap between Western attitudes toward Russia and those of countries in the "Global South," including Mexico, Malaysia, Algeria and Nigeria, where a much more favorable view of Moscow continues to predominate.[44]

A FORCE MULTIPLIER FOR RUSSIAN FOREIGN POLICY

As the foregoing suggests, disinformation plays an integral part in Russia's contemporary strategy, shoring up and augmenting Moscow's geopolitical initiatives. This is so for good reason. As Russia scholar Donald Jensen has explained:

> For all of Russia's weaknesses as a great power, Putin believes that it has one key advantage in its long-term competition with the United States and NATO: that Russia is more cohesive internally,

---

44 Latana/Alliance of Democracies, *Democracy Perceptions Index* 2023, May 2023, https://6389062.fs1. hubspotusercontent-na1.net/hubfs/6389062/Canva%20 images/Democracy%20Perception%20Index%202023.pdf.

and thus able to outlast its techno-
logically-superior but culturally- and
politically-pluralistic opponents. In recent
years, the Kremlin has used coercion,
misinformation and other disruptive
strategies to spread chaos, with the goal
of creating an environment in which the
side that copes best with such chaos (that
is, the one which is less susceptible to
societal disruption) wins. In other words,
Putin believes that Russia can endure in
a clash of civilizations by splintering its
opponents' alliances, dividing adversaries
internally, and undermining their political
systems while consolidating its own
population, resources, and cultural base.
Such a strategy avoids competing in
those areas where Russia is weak in hopes
of ensuring that, when confrontation
does come, Russia will enjoy a more level
playing field.[45]

Disinformation, in other words, represents an
essential asymmetric strategy for Moscow. It provides the Kremlin a low cost, indirect alternative

---

45 Donald N. Jensen, "Russia's Disinformation Offensive," in Ilan
    Berman, ed., *Digital Dictators: Media, Authoritarianism, and
    America's New Challenge* (Rowman & Littlefield, 2016), 26.

to actual military confrontation with the West – a confrontation that, should it actually occur, Moscow would find itself poorly positioned to compete in, in both strategic and economic terms.[46] It also permits Moscow to achieve a key strategic objective: to diminish the cohesion of the West, while simultaneously undermining trust in democratic institutions among key constituencies.[47] It is likewise central to advancing Russia's preferred narrative, and debunking alternative interpretations of world events, during times of crisis.

All of this helps to explain why the discipline of disinformation has not only endured in Russian doctrine but continued to grow in both scope and sophistication. The results represent a real, sustained and serious threat to open societies and democratic institutions alike.

---

46 Kim R. Holmes, "Putin's Asymmetrical War Against the West," *Foreign Policy*, May 5, 2014, https://foreignpolicy.com/2014/05/05/putins-asymmetrical-war-on-the-west/.

47 This objective was central to Russia's interference in the 2016 U.S. Presidential election. Russian efforts in this arena "represent the most recent expression of Moscow's longstanding desire to undermine the US-led liberal democratic order, but these activities demonstrated a significant escalation in directness, level of activity, and scope of effort compared to previous operations," a declassified 2017 assessment by the U.S. intelligence community judged. See Office of the Director of National Intelligence, *Assessing Russian Activities and Intentions in Recent US Elections*, January 6, 2017, https://www.scribd.com/document/335886615/Assessing-Russian-Activities-and-Intentions-in-Recent-US-Elections#.

MAPPING THE WESTERN RESPONSE

In Europe, Russia's 2014 invasion of Ukraine and its subsequent occupation of the Crimean Peninsula served as a long-overdue wake-up call about the dangers posed by persistent Russian imperialism, as well as the narratives and tropes that undergird it. For much of the preceding three decades, European policymakers had sought to engage post-Soviet Russia through a range of political and economic overtures. These involved a great number of things, ranging from the elevation of Russia's voice in NATO planning (exemplified by the creation of the NATO-Russia Council in the early 2000s) to more conciliatory economic policies and political arrangements. Through these steps, policymakers sought to mollify, accommodate and otherwise manage relations with Russia in a way that permitted them to expand the European "zone of peace."

This optimism, it should be noted, was not uniform. For the countries of Eastern Europe, which had directly experienced the predations of the Kremlin over the preceding century, skepticism regarding the feasibility of rehabilitating Russia abounded. To these nations, the concept of a Russia at peace with its neighbors was decidedly more tenuous – and the threat posed by the Kremlin more real – than it was to their counterparts. These more cautious views, however, were generally marginalized in a European debate that emphasized normalization of relations, and expanded trade, with Moscow.

Russia's 2014 aggression therefore came as a profound shock to a European community that had become convinced that some form of *modus vivendi* with the Kremlin was in fact possible. That sentiment had grown significantly in preceding years, thanks in no small measure to what was widely seen in the West as a more moderate, pragmatic phase of Russian policy, corresponding roughly to the presidency of Dmitry Medvedev (2008-2012).[48] The return of Vladimir Putin to the Russian presidency in 2012, however, brought with it an overt resurgence of expansionist tendencies on the part of the Kremlin, culminating in Moscow's decision to intervene in response to Ukraine's winter 2013 Maidan Revolution in an attempt to forestall Kyiv's pursuit of a Euro-Atlantic trajectory.

Russia's military campaign against Ukraine was punctuated by asymmetry. The tactics it employed ranged from use of irregular warfare (most directly through its employment of mercenaries – so called "little green men") to its encouragement of separatist tendencies in Ukrainian regions like Luhansk and Donetsk. Among the most prominent tactics harnessed by the Kremlin, however, was the use of disinformation. The 2014 Ukraine invasion, the scholar Marcel Van Herpen has written, was accompanied by the "most massive and incisive

---

48 Medvedev's more measured political rhetoric and conciliatory foreign policy stance sparked hopes of a "reset" with Washington, something that was pursued unsuccessfully by the Obama administration during its time in office. See, for instance, "Medvedev Says He Sees Chance For Better U.S. Ties," Reuters, November 18, 2008, https://www.rferl.org/a/Russias_Medvedev_Says_He_Sees_Chance_For_Better_US_Ties/1350422.html. Similar sentiments prevailed in Europe, with the European Union actively pursuing political compromise with the Kremlin during Medvedev's tenure. See, for instance, "Pragmatism prevails at EU-Russia summit," *EURACTIV*, June 1, 2010, https://www.euractiv.com/section/justice-home-affairs/news/pragmatism-prevails-at-eu-russia-summit/.

propaganda offensive of the past seventy years" on the part of the Kremlin.[49] The objectives of this assault were manifold. At home, it was intended to depict Ukraine as a wayward territory that needed to be rejoined to the Fatherland. In Ukraine, it was aimed at the demoralization of the population and, if possible, its mobilization against the country's government.[50] And beyond, it was designed to style Ukraine's government as fascist and in league with the West – part of a larger coordinated strategy to diminish Russia's global stature that needed to be thwarted.[51]

This informational offensive, in turn, proved effective in the opening stages of Russia's invasion and occupation of Crimea. Arguably, however, it had even more impact as the conflict transformed into a long-running asymmetric struggle – one in which Russian information manipulation helped to, among other things, perpetuate and amplify

---

49 Van Herpen, *Putin's Propaganda Machine: Soft Power and Russian Foreign Policy*, 1.

50 John R. Haines, "Russia's Use of Disinformation in the Ukraine Conflict," Foreign Policy Research Institute, February 17, 2015, https://www.fpri.org/article/2015/02/russias-use-of-disinformation-in-the-ukraine-conflict/.

51 Jensen, "Russia's Disinformation Offensive," in Berman, ed., *Digital Dictators: Media, Authoritarianism, and America's New Challenge*, 26.

separatist narratives in Ukraine's east and sow distrust in the country's citizenry.[52]

In response, Western nations began to erect a countervailing architecture of national agencies, initiatives and bureaucracies intended specifically to respond to the Russian informational threat. Nearly a decade on, this structure has evolved in interesting and important ways. The <u>eight</u> case studies below, while not a comprehensive picture of the counter-disinformation architecture created in the West in recent years, provide a representative sampling of the different "models" adopted by assorted Western governments in grappling with the threat of Russian disinformation, propaganda, and information manipulation.

The approaches vary widely, in terms of both scope and effectiveness. In aggregate, they paint a picture of an evolving and still imperfect response to what is increasingly seen as an existential challenge to the Western political order. As such, they hold a number of important lessons for the United States

---

52 Julia Summers, "Countering Disinformation: Russia's Infowar in Ukraine," University of Washington Henry M. Jackson School of International Studies, October 25, 2017, https://jsis.washington.edu/news/russia-disinformation-ukraine/.

in its own struggle to understand, and counteract, Russia's malign political and ideological influence.

THE EU: REGULATING THE THREAT

Although Russia's 2014 invasion of Ukraine woke European policymakers up to the danger of persistent Russian imperialism, nearly a decade on the movement to tackle the threat posed by Russia's information warfare, as well as that of other actors (such as China), is still nascent in nature – at least at the continent-wide level. Bureaucratically, the EU's counter-disinformation infrastructure remains modest in scope, centered on the East StratCom Task Force of the European External Action Service (EEAS), the EU's equivalent of a foreign ministry. However, although the Task Force represents the EU's principal mechanism focusing on countering foreign disinformation in its various forms, it remains a fledgling organization in many ways. As of Fall 2022, it employed just thirteen staff members, and – according to its officials – lacked the budget and resources to spearhead a truly continent-wide coordinating effort against foreign (mainly Russian) information warfare.[53]

    This, however, could be changing. In the wake

---

53 Author interviews, Brussels, Belgium, October 2022.

of the February 2022 Russian invasion of Ukraine, the question of disinformation has "migrated from the margins of the foreign policy debate into the mainstream," in the words of one EU official.[54] As a result, there is now sustained top-level attention from the European Commission, Europe's top coordinating and administrative body, on the need to counter what its officials classify as Foreign Interference and Malign Influence (FIMI).

What form that will take remains to be seen. EEAS officials are hopeful that more attention from bureaucrats in Brussels will allow them to shunt greater resources into efforts like East Stratcom's "Rapid Alert System" (RAS), a coordinating mechanism intended to share best practices and emerging disinformation trends with a growing network of governments and NGOs throughout the EU – as well as across the Atlantic. They maintain that this mechanism holds considerable merit, in that it allows member states to "pre-bunk" emerging disinformation narratives. They point to the October 2022 effort by Russia to generate a false story about Ukraine's willingness to use a "dirty bomb" (a narrative that was roundly and

---

54 Ibid.

publicly rejected by the EU and the U.S.[55]) as a proof of concept for how the RAS could prove useful in informing policy in the future. Such instances, however, remain the exception rather than the norm; according to observers, the RAS is still largely conceptual, with lackluster information sharing and only sporadic engagement from constituent governments and non-governmental organizations.[56]

Concurrently, Europe has focused its efforts on a related effort, one with the power to dramatically reshape discourse on the continent. The EU's much-discussed *Digital Services Act* (DSA), a signature initiative of current European Commission President Ursula von der Leyen, is designed to "create a safer digital space" and provide enhanced protections for European internet users. It aims to do so by "harmonizing" assorted national level laws – such as those that currently prevail in Germany and Austria – and applying them across the length and breadth of the Eurozone. The DSA contains, among other things, provisions designed to compel better content moderation

---

55   "Western Allies Reject Russia's Claim That Ukraine Plans To Use 'Dirty Bomb' To Escalate War," *Radio Free Europe/ Radio Liberty*, October 24, 2022, https://www.rferl.org/a/ blinken-ukraine-dirty-bomb-shoigu/32097955.html.

56   Author interviews, Brussels, Belgium, October 2022.

by social media platforms and big tech firms, as well as greater transparency as to the functioning of their algorithms. The Act entered into force in November of 2022. Internet service providers now have until January of 2024 to bring their activities in line with its provisions.

Notably, this effort is intended, at least in part, to address the spread of disinformation and "harmful content." The DSA includes a strengthened (albeit voluntary) code of practice which commits signatories to "demonetising the dissemination of disinformation; ensuring the transparency of political advertising; empowering users; enhancing the cooperation with fact-checkers; and providing researchers with better access to data."[57] European officials are bullish that this framework will provide added protections and monitoring against Russian-driven disinformation, although they admit that the Code may not be applicable in the United States, which possesses a different – and stronger – stance on the freedom of speech than that which prevails in Europe.

Policymakers in Brussels are also focusing locally. In the wake of Russia's February 2022

---

57 European Commission, "The 2022 Code of Practice on Disinformation," n.d., https://digital-strategy.ec.europa.eu/en/policies/code-practice-disinformation.

invasion of Ukraine, European Commission President Ursula von der Leyen announced that the Eurozone would ban Russian state propaganda outlets RT and *Sputnik*.[58] European Union members have now followed through on that decision, with both outlets banned from broadcasting on television and satellite providers, and their content blocked on social media platforms such as Twitter accessible to Europeans. In the wake of this change, new attention is being paid to the need to message to the millions of Russian-language speakers now resident within the European Union.

Existing mechanisms of doing so are seen as deeply deficient. The Russian-language channel of France-based European television network *Euronews* is broadly looked upon with disdain by European officials, who fault its lackluster programming and poor production values for its current, marginal status. As a result, there are now nascent efforts underway to establish supplemental means of outreach to this target audience. For instance, Vera Jourova, the EC's Vice President for Values and Transparency, has proposed the creation of a *Radio Free Russia* to bring fresh media and news

---

58   Laura Kayali, "EU to ban Russia's RT, Sputnik media outlets, von der Leyen says," *Politico*, February 27, 2022, https://www.politico.eu/article/ursula-von-der-leyen-announces-rt-sputnik-ban/.

content to Russians now residing in Europe, as well as to amplify the efforts of Russian exile media.[59] (Notably, the EU's decision to ban Russian state media from its airwaves is itself not without controversy; experts and researchers indicate that, in the wake of the edict, it has become "harder to see" and track Russian propaganda efforts – something that is necessary in order to martial responses to false narratives being promulgated by the Kremlin and its proxies.[60])

Much of the current momentum in European policy is undergirded by extensive support for, and solidarity with, Ukraine in its ongoing fight against Russian aggression. A year-and-a-half into the Ukraine war, European politicians and institutions remain consolidated in their backing of Kyiv, as well as their view of the conflict as a broad, ideological struggle for primacy with the Kremlin. However, there are clear efforts by Russia and Russian-aligned misinformation actors to chip away at this consensus through the promotion of divisive themes and narratives intended to amplify

---

59 Jennifer Rankin, "Senior EU official calls for a 'Radio Free Russia' to help exiled media," *Guardian*, January 23, 2023, https://www.theguardian.com/world/2023/jan/27/senior-eu-official-calls-for-a-radio-free-russia-to-help-exiled-media.

60 Author interviews, Brussels, Belgium, October 2022.

domestic discontent in the European Union's constituent parts.

THE CZECH REPUBLIC: BUILDING A WALLED GARDEN

While the Czech Republic is often portrayed in Western discourse as a leader in the field of countering disinformation, the actual state of play within the country itself is both more nuanced and more tenuous. Like elsewhere in Europe, the contemporary field of counter-disinformation in the Czech Republic got its start in the wake of Russia's 2014 invasion of Ukraine and subsequent occupation of Crimea. Following those events, the Czech government took early steps toward erecting a national counter-disinformation enterprise, although momentum was hampered by the disinterest of the administration of former Prime Minister Andrej Babis, and greatly complicated by the historically pro-Russian positions and entanglements of its then-president, Milos Zeman.

Nevertheless, several notable milestones did take place. In 2016, the government conducted a National Security Audit that assessed ten threat categories and the state's capacity to respond to them. Among other objectives, the Audit mapped out the steps needed to implement a serious government-wide counter-disinformation effort. Relatedly, the Audit laid the foundation for the establishment of a hybrid threats center in the country's Ministry of Interior the following year. That unit continues to operate, and as of Fall 2022 employed some ten professionals whose work focuses on tracking hybrid or "asymmetric" threats – including disinformation – within the country. It also serves as a coordination hub of sorts, working with other government units to track, identify and, when needed, debunk and/or contextualize misleading media narratives.

The problem they confront has unique characteristics. In comparative terms, the Czech disinformation ecosystem is small. Like elsewhere in the EU, Russian state media channels are banned (although the Czech-language version of Russia's *Sputnik* continues to operate, and – as in other European nations – is freely accessible to anyone with a virtual private network [VPN]). As a consequence, the main disinformation actors active in the country are the estimated 30-40 websites that transmit and amplify pro-Russian themes, stories and narratives, and which in turn acquire significant traction on social media.[61] Notably, rather than seeding qualitatively new narratives into the Czech information eco-system, Russian- and Russian-aligned actors have tended to focus on issues of domestic concern to ordinary citizens, such as rising energy prices, growing worries about the economy, and distrust of Ukrainian immigrants and of the European Union writ large. At least some of these disinformation actors are organic and home-grown, driven by financial gain rather than ideological commitment to the Kremlin. In many ways, as one observer put it, disinformation in the Czech Republic is a "business," and a rather lucrative one at that.[62]

Exacerbating the problem is the low level of media literacy within the country, which makes it difficult for the citizenry to differentiate rep- utable and disreputable news sources and makes them more likely to share dis- or misinformation. Government officials consequently stress the value of an independent, well-regarded media organization – such as the country's Academy of Media Literacy – that can "rank" media sources in a way that in the future might assist search engines

---

61 Author's interviews, Prague, Czech Republic, October 2022.

62 Ibid.

and social media platforms to steer users to more credible sources of information.[63]

As elsewhere, Russia's February 2022 invasion of Ukraine kicked Czech counter-disinformation efforts into significantly higher gear. In March 2022, the government of new Prime Minister Petr Fiala appointed a Cabinet-level disinformation coordinator, Michal Klima, and empowered the creation of a new disinformation coordination unit under his direction headquartered in the Office of the Government of the Czech Republic. Officials in Prague subsequently began to consider a "wish list" of next steps, ranging from bigger budgets to greater manpower and new institutions, to further flesh out the Czech counter-disinformation enterprise.[64]

Missing, however, is what might be termed a fulsome official strategy undergirding this project. While governmental units (such as the Interior Ministry's hybrid threats center, and "stratcom" teams in the Czech Ministries of Foreign Affairs and Defense) continue to operate, these efforts remain siloed and, according to their members, are not effectively netted together in a broader vision of interagency and intragovernmental cooperation.[65]

---

63 Ibidem.

64 Author's interviews, Prague, Czech Republic, October 2022.

65 Ibid.

Absent, too, is a regulatory framework for governing state action against disinformation actors. In February 2022, following recommendations from the Czech government and intelligence services, the country's national domain operator de-platformed a number of websites identified as being involved in amplifying Russian disinformation. The action, while temporarily successful in staunching the transmission of pro-Kremlin narratives, generated a domestic furor about governmental overreach. As a result, officials in Prague say, the government needs a new law which could enable – and provide a structure for – future such actions, should they be taken.[66]

As the foregoing suggests, the Czech response to disinformation currently resembles what might best be termed a "walled garden." Czech authorities have pursued measures to insulate their population from the pernicious effects of Russian disinformation, relying on regulations promulgated by the European Union as well as some (not yet fully judicial) methods of their own. Having done so, Prague is now grappling with the legal challenges of confronting hostile actors operating within the domestic media space whose messaging

---

66 Ibidem.

aligns closely with that of a foreign adversary but is protected under free speech. Far less attention, however, is being paid to the broader Russian disinformation effort and its dominant narratives, tropes and impact on the region.

The limitations of this approach have become visible in recent months. In early 2023, the country's presidential election was beset by significant information-driven disruptions, among them false reports (discovered to have originated from Russia) that the leading candidate, Gen. Petr Pavel, had died.[67] Likewise, during the election season, false messages purporting to be from Pavel were sent to the cell phones of citizens announcing a general mobilization in support of Ukraine in an effort to sow distrust in government, and to turn public opinion against Pavel's candidacy.[68] As these incidents underscore, Russian disinformation today "is actively spreading in the Czech Republic in various

---

67 Anna Fodor, "False news of Pavel's death came from Russia but specific perpetrator not identified," *Radio Prague International*, February 6, 2023, https://english.radio.cz/false-news-pavels-death-came-russia-specific-perpetrator-not-identified-8784858.

68 "Čechům chodí falešné zprávy údajně od Petra Pavla o mobilizaci na Ukrajinu" [The Czechs are getting false news, allegedly from Petr Pavel, about the mobilization to Ukraine], Echo24, January 18, 2023, https://echo24.cz/a/Hby7N/zpravy-domaci-podvodne-falesne-sms-petr-pavel-prezidentske-volby-policie.

ways," despite the infrastructure erected so far by Prague to combat it.[69]

Meanwhile, that infrastructure is beginning to show alarming signs of erosion. In February 2023, in the wake of the country's national election, the post of governmental counter-disinformation coordinator was abruptly eliminated.[70] While the reasons for the move remain unclear, they appear to be tied to the Czech Republic's approach to the Ukraine war, which is said to have fundamentally reordered the government's budgetary priorities and policy focus. (The disinformation portfolio is being subsumed under that of the country's national security advisor, a post that was itself newly created, and its immediate future currently remains unclear.)[71] Paradoxically, then, Prague's focus on Russian aggression in

69 "Russian Disinformation Narratives in Czech Republic in January 2023," *Vox Ukraine*, February 22, 2023, https://voxukraine.org/en/russian-disinformation-narratives-in-czech-republic-in-january-2023-policy-brief-within-kremlin-watchers-movement-project.

70 Tomas Pika, "Vláda zrušila funkci vládního zmocněnce pro média Klímy. Agendu dezinformací převezme poradce Pojar" [The government canceled the function of government representative for media Klima. Advisor Pojar will take over the information agenda], iRozhlas, February 15, 2023, https://www.irozhlas.cz/zpravy-domov/michal-klima-zmocnenec-media-dezinformace-vlada-konec-tomas-pojar_2302151348_pik.

71 Tim Gosling, "Czech Republic: Efforts to fight disinformation grind to a halt," International Press Institute, April 20, 2023, https://ipi.media/czech-republic-efforts-to-fight-disinformation-grind-to-a-halt/.

Ukraine, which has been accompanied by extensive propaganda and disinformation, appears to have made it less, rather than more, attuned to the attendant penetration of Russian-driven disinformation within its own borders.

POLAND: A POLITICIZED RESPONSE

Given geographic proximity and a fraught Cold War history, Poland has long viewed Russia as the principal threat to its national security and independence.[72] Consequently, since the country's independence from the Soviet Union in 1989, successive governments in Warsaw have made combatting Russian political interference, including disinformation, a major national priority.

Russian disinformation directed toward Poland is similar in both form and purpose to that which targets its Eastern Bloc neighbors. Both long-running and consistent, it has sought to undermine Poland's reputation and international standing, as well as to weaken its relationships with other countries in its immediate neighborhood and

---

72 https://ndupress.ndu.edu/Media/News/News-Article-View/
    Article/3323942/polands-threat-assessment-deepened-
    not-changed/.

beyond.[73] Notably, both the volume and scope of Russian disinformation directed against Poland has increased significantly since the outbreak of the Ukraine conflict in February 2022, owing to Warsaw's emergence as a leading member of the Western coalition seeking to penalize and isolate the Kremlin for its war of conquest. Modern Russian narratives have sought to heighten tensions between Poland and its neighbors, as well as to diminish enthusiasm among its citizenry for participation in the conflict or the provision of refuge to Ukrainians displaced by the fighting.[74]

Poland's response to this informational threat has been to spread the counter-disinformation "mission" across a number of governmental agencies and institutions, each of which have assumed a measure of competency in addressing the challenge of Russian propaganda and fake news. These include:

- Poland's Ministry of National Defence (MON), which is responsible for tracking and combatting the information warfare activities of adversary nations;

---

73 Mikolaj Rogalewicz, "Russian Disinformation Against Poland and Ukraine," Warsaw Institute *Special Report*, February 2023, https://issuu.com/warsawinstitute/docs/rs_02-2023_ en_1_.

74 Ibid.

- The country's domestic security agency, the Internal Security Agency (ABW), which polices the domestic sphere for hostile and destabilizing activities, including disinformation campaigns and foreign-origin propaganda;

- Poland's Ministry of Foreign Affairs, which serves as Warsaw's principal liaison with foreign governments and organizations on issues relating to disinformation;

- Poland's Ministry of Education, which has primary competence for instilling resilience against foreign manipulation in the national population. The ministry accomplishes this both directly and by working in partnership with private sector organizations. (However, as critics have noted, the government as yet does not possess a coherent national strategy for fostering media literacy writ large, and is focusing its efforts primarily on digital literacy instead.[75])

---

75 See, for instance, Grzegorz Ptaszek, "Media Literacy in Poland," webinar presentation, n.d., https://cdn1.media-and-learning.eu/files/2021/02/Media-literacy-in-Poland.pdf.

- The National Broadcasting Council, a regulatory body tasked with overseeing the country's electronic media sector. The Council has played a key role in aligning Poland's media policies with those of the broader European Union. For instance, with the outbreak of the Ukraine war, it moved to de-register Russian broadcasters such as RT, Soyuz TV and *Rossiya 24* from national airwaves,[76] prefiguring European Commission President Ursula von der Leyen's subsequent call to ban Russian state media from the Eurozone.

Nevertheless, despite this distributed architecture, Poland's fight against Russian disinformation has been significantly complicated and clouded in recent years by internal political divisions. The 2015 victory of the conservative Law and Justice Party (PiS) in 2015 was followed by a governmental campaign against the country's public television and radio broadcasters – one that saw many media executives replaced, and which stoked both domestic and international worries that Warsaw was seeking

---

76 Government of Poland, National Broadcasting Council, "Russian programs removed from the registry of distributed programs," February 25, 2022, https://www.gov.pl/web/krrit-en/russian-programs-removed-from-the-registry-of-distributed-programs.

to bring national media to heel at the expense of press freedom.[77] The ongoing political dominance of the PiS in the years since, together with the party's increasingly intrusive efforts to reshape civil society, has had a negative impact on the overall vibrancy of the country's media. Poland has charted a multi-year decline in the press freedom rankings kept by Reporters Without Borders, falling to 66th place out of 180 nations surveyed in the 2022 edition of the group's *World Press Freedom Index*.[78] In its assessment, RSF accused the government of having turned the country's public media "into instruments of propaganda," and of attempting to "control information on sensitive subjects" in both private and public media outlets.[79]

This trend has persisted. The Polish government's response to the recent surge of Russian disinformation has once again stirred considerable domestic controversy, as well as concerns about democratic backsliding in the country. In the Spring of 2023, Poland's parliament passed, and Polish

---

77 See, for instance, Annabelle Chapman, "Pluralism Under Attack: The Assault on Press Freedom in Poland," Freedom House, 2017, https://freedomhouse.org/sites/default/files/2020-02/FH_Poland_Media_Report_Final_2017.pdf.

78 "Poland falls in World Press Freedom Index for seventh year running," *Notes from Poland*, May 4, 2022, https://notesfrompoland.com/2022/05/04/poland-falls-in-world-press-freedom-index-for-seventh-year-running/.

79 Ibid.

President Andrzej Duda subsequently signed into law, a new law designed to combat Russian influence. The measure establishes a state commission to investigate the country's "mass media" as well as opposition political parties for evidence of Russian interference. The scope and activities of the commission, which has extensive executive power and will be able to issue summonses to journalists and individuals suspected of relying on Russian sources, raised concerns among watchdog groups over the potential chilling effect on free media in the country as well as on national politics.[80] The Polish government has since made efforts to soften the law,[81] but the measure has nevertheless drawn rebukes from the European Union and opposition politicians, who see it as a potential threat to democratic principles.

In this way, the clarity of Poland's fight against Russian disinformation has been clouded by its own domestic politics, much to the detriment of a coherent national vision relating to the informational threat posed by Russia – or even a

---

80 Reporters Without Borders, "Press Freedom threatened by Poland's new commission on Russian influence," June 8, 2023, https://rsf.org/en/press-freedom-threatened-poland-s-new-commission-russian-influence.

81 "Polish president backpedals on law on undue Russian influence," Reuters, June 2, 2023, https://www.reuters.com/world/europe/polish-president-proposes-changes-law-undue-russian-influence-2023-06-02/.

societal consensus about its dangers. All of which has allowed Russian disinformation narratives to continue to adversely impact Polish society, with significant effect. In a recent survey commissioned by the Warsaw Enterprise Institute, 34 percent of respondents agreed with the idea that the Ukraine war represents "a liberal conspiracy by Western elites," while 41 percent supported the notion that "refugees from Ukraine are actually economic migrants."[82] Worryingly, the study authors note, these findings reflect a notable shift in attitudes toward "theses favorable to Putin's policies" in comparison to past surveys.[83]

LATVIA: OUTSOURCING AWARENESS AND RESPONSE

In Latvia, the strategic communications mission can be said to sit at the center of the governmental conversation. A dedicated "stratcom" unit, housed in the State Chancellery (the national equivalent of the office of the Prime Minister) was founded in 2020, and now oversees the government's work on media, disinformation and communications. This

---

82 "Crisis or Propaganda? Attitudes of Poles towards the war in Ukraine," Warsaw Enterprise Institute, January 2023, https://wei.org.pl/wp-content/uploads/2023/01/Crisis-or-Propaganda.pdf.

83 Ibid.

work includes formulating long-term strategy for the country in dealing with the disinformation phenomenon, and to that end Latvia's government released its "national concept" on strategic communications priorities for 2023-2027 in the Spring of 2023.[84]

That plan focuses on three main pillars: 1) government communications, 2) fostering quality journalism, and 3) civic resilience. Among the notable benchmarks and objectives contained in it is the goal of achieving media literacy for at least 75 percent of the country's nearly two million person population – something that, according to officials in Riga, will help expand national resiliency to Russian disinformation and malign influence.[85] They note that Latvia is not as advanced as its neighbors in integrating such training into its school curricula, and this will consequently be a major focus over the next half-decade under the new "national concept."[86]

Even so, the country has already chalked up some significant successes to date. Latvian officials

84 Government of Latvia, *The National Concept on Strategic Communication and Security of the Information Space* 2023-2027, January 24, 2023, https://www.mk.gov.lv/en/media/15446/download?attachment.

85 Author's interviews, Riga, Latvia, February 2023.

86 Ibid.

credit these victories to the government's emphasis on tracking (and countering) the *methods* of foreign malign influence, rather than focusing on identifying and rebutting specific narratives and stories.[87] Nevertheless, they lament that the current Latvian counter-disinformation enterprise is as yet not fully formed. Nor is it the preferred national approach of a "whole of government" response, complete with multiple agencies and stakeholders as well as a central coordinating mechanism that doesn't change with the political tides. According to policymakers in Riga, resources for a robust national counter-disinformation effort are lacking, making countering foreign (mainly Russian) propaganda still something of an "unfunded mandate."[88]

As a consequence, Latvia's government has come to rely on external players to augment its response. For instance, Latvia lacks a robust early warning/monitoring mechanism through which to track and assess Russian disinformation activities. Instead, it relies on NATO's Strategic Communications Center of Excellence (COE), which is headquartered in Riga, to fulfill that function. The NATO COE plays a critical role for the Alliance

---

87 Ibidem.

88 Author's interviews, Riga, Latvia, February 2023.

in monitoring the informational space and the activities of hostile actors such as Russia, China and terrorist groups, and Riga depends significantly on this capability to alert it to emerging narratives, threats and malicious informational actors.

At the same time, Latvia has come to depend on its status as a hub for Russian opposition media to communicate with its own sizeable Russian-speaking diaspora. The weeks after the Russian invasion of Ukraine saw a massive tightening of the Latvian information sphere, with the government in Riga instituting a comprehensive ban on Russian channels like RTR and *Ren TV*, which had previously occupied prominent roles in the country's media environment. These were replaced by more programming from indigenous Latvian channels, by content from the West (such as Radio Free Europe/ Radio Liberty's *Current Time* channel), and other sources. However, an increasingly prominent role is being played by the growing number of Russian exile media outlets active in the country. This activity is not without its tensions.[89] However, in the main, authorities in Riga appear comfortable with

89 A notable example is the case of the *Dozhd* television channel, which ran afoul of Latvian authorities in late 2022 as a result of coverage deemed overly sympathetic to Russia. *Dozhd* had its license revoked by Latvia's state media regulator as a result, forcing it to begin the process of repositioning to The Netherlands.

their country serving as an informational haven for Russian opposition media, for both strategic and domestic political purposes.

ESTONIA: BUILDING CAPACITY

Like its Baltic neighbors, Estonia is pursuing a "whole of government" approach to informational threats and the disinformation environment. In this effort, strategic communication is seen as a "brick in the wall" in defending the country against foreign manipulation. The Estonian model has been in formation for some time, but has been refined and perfected as a result of the Ukraine war.[90] It now consists of six elements:

> **Shuttering of Russian media.** Unlike other European nations, Russian media was largely free and unregulated in Estonia prior to the outbreak of the Ukraine war. With the start of the conflict in February 2022, however, the Estonian government acted almost immediately to shut down the Russian-language information space by formally banning outlets such as *Sputnik* and *RT*.

---

90 Author's interviews, Tallinn, Estonia, February 2023.

(However, as elsewhere, these media sources remain accessible to individuals via VPNs.)

Creation of indigenous Russian media.
With the blocking of Russian media outlets, the Estonian government invested in the creation of indigenous media channels that broadcast in Russian as a way of maintaining engagement with the country's sizeable (~300,000) Russian and Russian-speaking population. These channels continue to operate, but do so under the broader social compact that prevails within the country – as well as clear guidelines about what content is, and isn't, appropriate.

Education about Russian disinformation.
The Estonian government has invested heavily in support of universities, NGOs and other entities in an effort to build awareness of, and resilience against, Russian disinformation methods. This has included "youth media" camps designed to instill critical thinking, as well as media literacy courses in primary and secondary schools. In collaboration with the University of Tartu, the Estonian government is now standing up a certificate program to foster disinformation

expertise and professionalization. This effort, which is being partially underwritten by the United States, is intended to attract international participants as well in what Estonian officials hope will become a sustained effort to build global expertise in the counter-disinformation space.

Exposing disinformation. The Estonian government actively works with journalists, provides support for relevant NGOs and watchdog groups, carries out "fact checks" to debunk false or misleading narratives, and provides situational awareness briefs to politicians and public figures.

Organization. The Estonian government actively curates the national cyberspace, and officials (law enforcement and otherwise) are empowered to tackle issues such as cyber-bullying, as well as interfacing with "Big Tech" and social media companies.

Regulation. Here, the Estonian government follows the lead of the European Union, focusing on implementation of the *Digital Services Act* and the associated "Code of Practice" against disinformation.

Additionally, Estonia's government – working in collaboration with the University of Tartu – has developed an innovative "social penetration model."[91] This effort examines disinformation narratives across several indices (virality, engagement, etc.) to help determine which tropes and messages need to be most urgently debunked or dispelled. In such a way, the Estonian government hopes to optimize its "rapid reaction" response and nip disinformation in the bud, before it has a chance to take hold in society.

Nevertheless, while undeniably robust, these efforts are not necessarily self-sustaining. Government officials in Tallinn admit that their counter-disinformation work is not fully funded solely at home, and they continue to rely on foreign funds (from the EU and U.S.) for continued functioning.[92] As they indicate, without such sustained support from external sources, it is not clear whether the counter-disinformation mission, although a clear priority for the Estonian government, would continue to function as needed.

---

91 Ibid.

92 Ibidem.

LITHUANIA: ALL HANDS ON DECK

The Baltic nation of Lithuania has what is arguably the most robust infrastructure for countering Russian disinformation of all contemporary nations faced with the Kremlin's information manipulation practices. That effort spans the nation's armed forces, multiple ministries, assorted governmental agencies and entities, and beyond. The aggregate result is an infrastructure that extends beyond the "whole of government" approach that its neighbors aspire to, and includes critical stakeholders in Lithuanian civil society as well.

The Lithuanian armed forces, for instance, established their dedicated "stratcom" unit as long ago as 2010 to observe "hostile" influence on society. The effort has matured considerably since, and now represents a core competency of the Lithuanian military. The Lithuanian armed forces define this mission as: observing the informational environment; coordinating responses to hostile informational activities; public affairs; public events; and "patriotic education." Lithuanian military officials view every citizen as a "warrior," and warn that if he or she is not armed intellectually and actively messaged to and engaged by the government, they could become vulnerable "to manipulation by the other side."[93] For them, Russian disinformation objectives have a clear purpose. At home, Russia is attempting "to increase the will to obey." Within Lithuania and other target nations, Russia tries "to reduce the will to resist," via tactics such as delegitimization, as well as fomenting cultural and societal tensions. In the West, meanwhile, Russia seeks "to reduce the will to defend" against its ideological encroachment.[94]

Beyond the military, "stratcom" units reside in multiple governmental agencies, including the country's Ministries of Foreign Affairs and Interior. All of these entities are coordinated by the National Crisis Management Centre, a sort of fusion center headquartered in the professional offices of the ruling government. The Centre is responsible for making decisions about which narratives need to be reacted to, and by whom. Its officials emphasize that "picking the proper messenger" is crucial, and great care is taken to identifying the department/agency/actor that is best positioned to "scope" the issue properly when an incident occurs. As they note, a governmental response is not always best,

---

93 Author's interviews, Vilnius, Lithuania, February 2023.

94 Ibid.

especially given that overall trust in government (at around 36 percent) remains low.[95]

Functionally, the Centre holds weekly gatherings with government officials responsible for the strategic communications portfolio, as well as key elements in the country's print, broadcast and digital media sectors, in order to "align" narratives and establish a working framework for contextualizing events and developments to the citizenry. Officials there make clear that the Centre is intended as a rapid reaction mechanism, and is beholden to a 2020 governmental order that stipulates that disinformation narratives must be responded to within two hours of them occurring. Notably, funding and manpower for this effort are increasing. Officials say that staffing has "doubled" over the past year, as a result of a surge of activity and readiness stemming from the Ukraine war.[96]

What sets the Lithuanian "model" apart is the extensive involvement of the country's civil society and economic sectors in the counter-disinformation mission. This is evident in at least two concrete ways. Educationally, the country is considerably

---

95 Ibidem.

96 Author's interviews, Vilnius, Lithuania, February 2023.

more mature than its neighbors in "professionaliz-ing" its bureaucrats and specialists to a competency in information warfare. For several years now, Vilnius University has offered a graduate level track designed to build strategic communications and disinformation expertise. At the same time, the country's media conglomerates have become active participants in debunking and countering Russian propaganda. For instance, Delfi, Lithuania's largest television channel and digital content provider, has independently aired programs like "Lie Detector," designed to contextualize news stories and elimi-nate falsehoods, for a number of years now.[97]

This infrastructure is significantly reinforced by the fact that Lithuania remains an active target of Russian information warfare. According to offi-cials, Moscow has maintained an active schedule of disinformation attacks on Lithuania in recent years, and last year roughly 5,000 such attacks, focused on topics such as the war in Ukraine, NATO, the Nord Stream II pipeline, nuclear rhetoric, and so on, were registered.[98] The goals of these and other efforts,

---

97 See, for instance, *"Delfi's Lie Detector* – the best fact-checking success story in Europe, to be introduced at international Facebook event," delfi.lt, January 15, 2021, https://www.delfi.lt/en/business/delfi-s-lie-detector-the-best-fact-checking-success-story-in-europe-to-be-introduced-at-international-facebook-event-86237847.

98 Author's interviews, Vilnius, Lithuania, February 2023.

broadly speaking, is to reduce the confidence of citizens in the competence of their government and undermine support for NATO and the EU. Notably, however, they also mark an evolution of the messaging themes and narratives being employed by Russian disinformation actors. Pre-2014, Russian disinformation targeted Lithuanian history, culture, and the domestic energy situation. Since the start of the Ukraine war, however, the messaging has focused largely on external issues, such as the inherent dangers of being part of NATO and EU. In terms of objectives, Lithuanian officials say, the Russians are seeking 1) to convince people that Lithuania is a failed state, so that it returns to Russia – or at least to its geopolitical orbit; 2) to convince Lithuanians that NATO membership represents a threat to their country, in order to diminish support for the Alliance, leading to an exit from the bloc; and 3) to convince Lithuanians that the EU is falling apart, so that they lessen their support for, and ultimately abandon, the project.[99]

Fundamentally, Lithuania's "whole of society" approach works because Russian disinformation is viewed as an "existential threat" to the nation, and everyone is united in the understanding that they

---

99 Ibid.

must work to defeat/debunk the "breakdown" narrative promoted by Russian and Russian-aligned informational actors.[100] This response is also deeply rooted in Lithuania's strategic culture. The country sees itself as the "Silicon Valley" of Europe's democracy movement, and aspires to be the pro-freedom hub in the region. Officials in Vilnius point with pride to the fact that a number of Russian opposition elements (including the "teams" of jailed Kremlin critic Alexei Navalny and opposition figure Gary Kasparov) have made Vilnius their headquarters. This role is not without conflict, however, and observers anticipate intensified jockeying for position among these groups and others (both Belarusian and Ukrainian) as this movement becomes more mature. Indeed, they "welcome it," in the words of one observer, because of what it would suggest about the vibrancy of democratic impulses, given that freedom has been in steady decline globally in recent years.[101]

SWEDEN: A COUNTER-DISINFORMATION "QUARTERBACK"

Sweden's response to Russian disinformation centers on the country's Psychological Defence

---

100 Ibidem.

101 Author's interviews, Vilnius, Lithuania, February 2023.

Agency. The Agency, which was stood up in the wake of Russia's 2014 invasion of Crimea as part of the country's Civil Contingencies Ministry, was more recently spun off as an independent/autonomous agency under the auspices of the Ministry of Defence. It began operations in its current form on January 1, 2022, and its mission and priorities were reinforced soon thereafter by Russia's invasion of Ukraine. The Agency currently employs approximately 50 specialists. However, its officials say, both the staff and budget are growing as the Swedish government becomes increasingly invested in the Agency's "mission set."[102]

That mission includes: raising awareness of disinformation threats (through lectures, briefings and other educational activities); monitoring the information space and alerting government agencies/actors to new and emerging threats; and enabling parallel/augmenting research into the phenomenon (by funding academic studies and the activities of aligned researchers). As such, the Agency represents a comparatively serious, well-funded approach to disinformation – and one with a broad mandate and extensive trust in governmental circles.

Notably, the Psychological Defence Agency

---

102 Author's interviews, Stockholm, Sweden, February 2023.

serves another function as well. It acts as the central coordinating hub for government-wide counter-disinformation activities resident in the country's other Ministries and branches. It also operates as the principal vehicle for Stockholm's outreach to, and interaction with, other countries carrying out work in the counter-disinformation space, including extensive collaboration with relevant Baltic agencies and units.[103]

Nevertheless, Sweden's resilience has been tested over the past year by a deluge of Kremlin-backed propaganda in response to its May 2022 decision, together with Finland, to abandon decades of neutrality and join the NATO alliance. Russian disinformation has sought to damage Sweden's international image, to highlight divisive themes (like controversial Koran burnings in Stockholm), and to dampen enthusiasm for membership in the bloc within Swedish society.[104] After considerable delay, Sweden began the process of formally joining the Alliance in July 2023, once it extended a

---

103 Ibid.

104 "Disinformation Narratives Related to Sweden and Finland's NATO Applications," Soufan Center *IntelBrief*, February 9, 2023, https://thesoufancenter.org/intelbrief-2023-february-9/; "Sweden says it's target of Russia-backed disinformation over NATO, Koran burnings," Reuters, July 26, 2023, https://www.reuters.com/world/europe/sweden-says-its-target-russia-backed-disinformation-over-nato-koran-burnings-2023-07-26/.

number of concessions to NATO member Turkiye. However, Russian disinformation directed against Stockholm has continued. In August 2023, the country's Psychological Defence Agency accused the Kremlin of disseminating Arabic-language falsehoods about official support for Koran burning in order to derail Sweden's accession process, as well as to stoke broader tensions between the Muslim World and the West.[105]

FINLAND: INSTILLING RESILIENCY

Among existing European responses to disinformation, that of Finland stands out. For roughly a decade, the country has been engaged in an intensive, multi-sector effort to inoculate its population from false information, and to empower citizens to effectively counter such fake narratives when they arise.[106] This contemporary strategy has its roots in a protracted struggle against Kremlin propaganda – one that stretches back to the country's declaration of independence from Moscow in

---

105 Miranda Bryant, "Russia spreading false claims about Qur'an burnings to harm Nato bid, says Sweden," *The Guardian*, August 6, 2023, https://www.theguardian.com/world/2023/aug/06/russia-spreading-false-claims-about-quran-burnings-to-harm-nato-bid-says-sweden.

106 Eliza Macintosh, "Finland is winning the war on fake news. What it's learned may be crucial to Western democracy," CNN, May 2019, https://edition.cnn.com/interactive/2019/05/europe/finland-fake-news-intl/

December of 1917. Nevertheless, this longstanding line of effort has been upgraded in recent years in response to Russia's changing disinformation tactics and modalities. It relies on several principles.

The first is the sharing of information regarding Russian disinformation across the breadth of the Finnish governmental bureaucracy. A number of governmental agencies in Helsinki have competency in, and jurisdiction over, the counter-disinformation portfolio. These include, most prominently, the Finnish Security Intelligence Service (SUPO), as well as the country's Ministry of Foreign Affairs and the Finnish Defense Forces. An important ancillary role is played by the Emergency Services Department of the country's Interior Ministry, which is responsible for analysis, crisis communications and preparedness relating to information warfare.

The second, and most widely known, is media literacy, which has become a major fixture in Finnish society. The country's educational system includes an extensive contemporary curriculum designed to teach citizens to identify false information from an early age.[107] This media literacy effort has become ubiquitous; as one recent report noted, "In the last

---

107 See, for instance, Jenny Gross, "How Finland Is Teaching a Generation to Spot Misinformation," *New York Times*, January 10, 2023, https://www.nytimes.com/2023/01/10/world/europe/finland-misinformation-classes.html.

decade, media literacy built upon critical thinking has become a vital, mandated part of Finland's core national curriculum. Teachers integrate the concepts into every subject from K-12, meaning Finnish students are exposed to media literacy from the start of their education, forming a first line of defence against disinformation."[108] In this fashion, the Finnish government works to "inoculate" its citizenry from the pernicious effects of Russian disinformation. This effort, moreover, is still a work in progress; the country's National Agency for Education recently mapped out a new strategy to make the Finnish population the most media-literate in the world by the end of this decade.[109]

The third is civic and media engagement. In contrast to many other Western nations, the country's media enjoys a high degree of trust in society, with roughly three-quarters of citizens expressing faith in both print and digital media outlets.[110] This confidence is attributable to the proactive role

108 Yvonne Lau, "Finland's 'visionary' fight against disinformation teaches citizens to question what they see online," *National Observer*, May 16, 2023, https://www.nationalobserver.com/2023/05/16/news/finland-visionary-fight-disinformation-teaches-citizens-question-online.

109 "New strategy aims at closing childhood literacy gap in Finland," *Yle News*, November 16, 2021, https://yle.fi/a/3-12190069.

110 Gross, "How Finland Is Teaching a Generation to Spot Misinformation."

played by Finnish media outlets in curating the country's internal media space – identifying and debunking Russian disinformation and information manipulation as it arises. Notably, this work is more than merely defensive in nature, and Finland's media outlets have become "counterpunchers" in their own right. For instance, *Helsingin Sanomat*, the country's largest newspaper, has started circumventing media restrictions imposed by the Russian government by seeding news stories about the true state of the war in Ukraine in the popular video game "Counter Strike," where Russian users are likely to see them.[111]

The effectiveness of Finland's approach is widely recognized. The country has for years occupied the top slot in the Open Society Institute's survey of resiliency to misinformation, across a pool of 41 European nations.[112] Nevertheless, the durability of Finland's counter-disinformation activities has been tested by the Ukraine war, as a result of which the country chose to abandon its longstanding policy of military neutrality and

111 "Finnish newspaper hides news for Russians in video game," *The Japan Times*, May 4, 2023, https://www.japantimes.co.jp/news/2023/05/04/world/finnish-newspaper-news-for-russians-video-game/.

112 "How It Started, How It is Going: Media Literacy Index 2022," Open Society Institute – Bulgaria, October 12, 2022, https://osis.bg/?p=4243&lang=en.

apply to join NATO. (It formally did so in April of 2023). That decision was accompanied by a new deluge of Russian-driven disinformation geared, as in Sweden, toward stoking discord in Finnish society and undermining trust in governmental decisions. However, the effort proved underwhelming, both because of the inherently insular nature of the Finnish language, which makes messaging tricky for non-native speakers, and because of the resilience that has been successfully instilled in the country's population through education and critical thinking.[113]

LESSONS LEARNED... SO FAR

As the case studies above illustrate, nearly a decade after Russia's initial invasion of Ukraine, the Western response to the attendant threat posed by Russian disinformation remains imperfect and evolving. Nevertheless, across the West, the most successful experiences to date in identifying, and responding to, Russian-driven disinformation share a number of commonalities. These features can cumulatively serve as a guide to "best practices" in responding to disinformation, both emanating from Russia and more broadly.

---

113 Lau, "Finland's 'visionary' fight against disinformation teaches citizens to question what they see online."

RAPID RESPONSE. In recent years, working through its own state media, as well as proxy outlets, troll accounts and other mechanisms, Russia has deftly exploited today's fast-moving, crowded media environment to gain greater resonance for its information operations.[114] Disinformation, moreover, should be understood as an "ongoing conversation," with new stories, lines of efforts, and angles being disseminated constantly as global events unfold. Keeping up with this dynamic field requires Western governments to adopt a "campaign footing," with both the capacity and resources to respond to new disinformation attacks and narratives in real time. Those that have built the capacity to do so, such as Lithuania, have met with great success in muting the resonance of new disinformation narratives as they emerge.

COORDINATION. To marshal a cogent response to disinformation,

---

114 See generally, Thomas Rid, *Active Measures: The Secret History of Disinformation and Political Warfare* (Farrar, Straus and Giroux, 2020).

experience has shown that a central agency with authority over the broad range of activities associated with the portfolio is needed. In Sweden, that function is fulfilled by the Psychological Defence Agency of the country's Ministry of Defense. By contrast, countries that lack such an authoritative coordinating mechanism have often found themselves hampered by a lack of coordination and competing authorities among the various agencies with partial ownership of the counter-disinformation "mission."

WHOLE OF SOCIETY. For effective counter-disinformation, extensive buy in from across the government is frequently a prerequisite for success. More often than not, countries in which the disinformation mission is "siloed" in just one or two agencies struggle to formulate a cogent response to Russian-driven narratives. By contrast, those that exhibit a "whole of government" response fare considerably better. However, nations that exhibit a robust "whole of society" ecosystem, comprised of multiple government agencies as well as civil society and media actors, are the best positioned to respond comprehensively and nimbly to disinformation narratives and tropes as they arise. Useful examples in this regard include Lithuania and Finland.

RESILIENCE. History has shown that disinformation has the widest reach and greatest resonance in societies where media literacy is low, and where publics, as a result of insufficient education and awareness, are inclined to believe narratives promulgated by opaque sources. In such places, like Poland, governments have often struggled to properly inform their citizenry, neutralize pernicious information operations, and build public trust. In others that have emphasized identifying false information as part of their educational curricula (such as Finland), efforts to marginalize and debunk disinformation have met with significant success.

PROFESSIONALIZATION. By
its nature, counter-disinformation is
a long-term enterprise, and one that
necessitates a trained, disciplined cadre
of professionals to staff it. This, in turn,
requires the development of a dedicated
training curriculum designed to incubate
a dedicated cohort of strategic communications professionals that can occupy
relevant posts in the medium- to long-
term. Finland and Lithuania, for instance,
have made the development of such
expertise a significant priority, yielding
a robust training course from whose
graduates the government can draw in
prosecuting the counter-disinformation
mission. Estonia, meanwhile, is now in
the process of erecting precisely such an
educational structure.

TRUST IN GOVERNMENT. When it
comes to addressing the challenge posed
by Russian disinformation, the confidence of society is essential. In countries
with high levels of trust in government,

such as Finland, authorities enjoy broad latitude in prosecuting the counter-disinformation mission, and ordinary citizens act as responsible stakeholders in this enterprise. Nevertheless, even in countries that struggle with comparatively low governmental trust among the local populace (e.g., Lithuania), societal buy-in for the counter-disinformation "mission" is nonetheless possible provided there is a clear, cogent understanding of the nature of the disinformation threat confronting the nation. An associated requirement is for the public to be assured that the government organs in question are not unduly politicized and remain focused on the external threat posed by Russian disinformation (rather than being weaponized in the context of domestic politics by the government or party in power).

NEXT STEPS IN THE FIGHT AGAINST RUSSIAN DISINFORMATION

Moscow's 2014 invasion of Ukraine reawakened much of the world to the enduring threat posed by Russian imperialism, and to the attendant danger of Russian disinformation. Nearly a decade on, the problem remains as urgent as ever, against the backdrop of a new Russian war of aggression against Ukraine. Meanwhile, the disruptive potential of Russian information warfare has grown, as today's new, more interconnected media environment offers the Kremlin more opportunities than ever before to shape global perceptions, narratives and outcomes.[115]

---

115 Ibid. See also Haroon K. Ullah. *Digital World War: Islamists, Extremists, and the Fight for Cyber Supremacy* (New Haven, CT: Yale University Press, 2017).

The Western response to this challenge, however, remains very much a work in progress. In spite of years of institution building, the architecture that has been erected to confront the threat is still brittle and imperfect, as the foregoing pages show. Nevertheless, it contains important lessons by which the U.S. can optimize its own response to the challenge posed by Russian information manipulation, and help to upgrade the response of allied governments in the process.

REGAINING EXPERTISE IN RUSSIAN INFORMATION WARFARE

For the United States, the path to effectively countering Russian disinformation begins with reclaiming an accurate understanding of how, and to what ends, Moscow manipulates the information sphere. This is knowledge that the U.S. once possessed. By the latter half of the Cold War, thanks to the intellectual work of a cohort of dedicated scholars and practitioners, the U.S. national security establishment wielded a high degree of competency in understanding how Moscow sought to exploit the information domain to its advantage – and the narratives, outlets and mechanisms that it was most likely to use in order to do so. Equally importantly, the U.S. government made significant efforts, via reports, disclosures and Congressional hearings, to raise popular awareness of Soviet attempts to manipulate public opinion.[116] All of this improved the resiliency of the American public to Soviet disinformation and upgraded the effectiveness of America's efforts to combat the USSR's appeal on the world stage.

The years that followed the Soviet collapse, however, were accompanied by a distinct attrition of expertise in, and appreciation for, the potency and persistence of Russian "active measures." Throughout the 1990s and 2000s, the United States paid little attention to Moscow's maneuvers in the information domain, even as it dismantled its own public diplomacy and messaging capabilities – a process that one high-level governmental panel equated to "unilateral disarmament" in "the weapons of advocacy."[117] Nor did it give much heed to warnings from Russia's former satellites that the Kremlin was reinvigorating its informational activities.

---

116 Rid, Active Measures: *The Secret History of Disinformation and Political Warfare*, pp. 316-326.

117 *Changing Minds, Winning Peace: A New Strategic Direction for U.S. Public Diplomacy in the Arab & Muslim World* (Washington: Advisory Group on Public Diplomacy for the Arab and Muslim World, October 1, 2003), 13.

This has served as a recipe for strategic surprise. The United States was caught largely off guard by the extent of Moscow's meddling in American politics in the run-up to the 2016 elections. In the years since, it has struggled to formulate a cogent response to Russia's ongoing manipulation of the information sphere, hampered by bureaucratic inertia and a lack of contemporary competence in the Kremlin's "soft power" strategies. Put simply, American politicians and policymakers today don't possess an adequate understanding of Russian strategic culture, or of the tools that Moscow deploys to advance its geopolitical objectives short of war. They need to, if they are to become competitive in the "battle of ideas" against Moscow once more. To successfully combat Russian disinformation, the United States needs to reacquaint itself with Russian strategy, and how Moscow views peacetime as part of a continuum of conflict – one in which it is committed to deploying an array of tools, messaging among them, to promote its own worldview and denigrate those of others.

The costs of not doing so are high. Today, the U.S. and its partners in Europe have marshalled a robust economic and military response to Russia's "special military operation" in Ukraine – one that has helped Kyiv to successfully repel Russian aggression over the past year-and-a-half. However, they have done little of substance to counter the Kremlin's accompanying informational offensive. As a result, Moscow has been largely unfettered in its manipulation of global media to increase tensions within Western societies, and to reshape perceptions and public opinion, particularly in the developing world, in its favor.[118]

Such manipulation is liable to persist beyond the current conflict. Whatever the ultimate resolution of the Ukraine war, absent a fundamental change of regime in Moscow Russia will remain aggressive, expansionist and at ideological odds with the West.[119] A better contemporary understanding of the internal drivers and dynamics animating Russian foreign policy is required if the United States is to rebuild its ability to anticipate, and debunk, Russian disinformation.

---

118 See, for instance, Latana/Alliance of Democracies, *Democracy Perceptions Index* 2023.

119 Ilan Berman, "The Sources of Russian Conduct," *The Journal of Policy & Strategy* 2, iss. 3, August 2022, https://nipp.org/wp-content/uploads/2022/08/Berman-Analysis.pdf.

SCALING TO MEET THE DISINFORMATION CHALLENGE

It's a simple truism of politics that governmental priorities are reflected in budgeting and resources. Those programs and initiatives that receive sustained political attention, enjoy bureaucratic buy-in, and have clear mission-sets receive the resources necessary for their operations. Those which don't, simply do not. Measured by this metric, there is a glaring mismatch between the degree to which Russia prioritizes information warfare, and how much the West is spending to marshal a serious response to it.

The numbers tell the story. The Russian government's consistent, heavy focus on funding information operations speaks volumes about how important these activities are to the Kremlin's overall grand strategy and foreign policy activities. To wit, as of the second half of 2022, Russia's "white budget" expenditures on foreign media manipulation were estimated to total more than $1.5 billion annually, despite the extensive raft of Western sanctions that have been leveled at Moscow over its war in Ukraine.[120] When the

---

120 Aleksandra Michalowska-Kubs and Jakob Kubs, "Coining lies. Kremlin spends 1.5 Billion per year to spread disinformation and propaganda," Debunk.org, August 8, 2022, https://www.debunkeu.org/coining-lies-state-budget-financing-of-russian-propaganda

activities of Kremlin-aligned media actors, like oligarch and Wagner Group founder Yevgeny Prigozhin, are taken into account, that total is believed to be closer to $2.4 billion per year.[121] (Prigozhin's abortive June 2023 mutiny against the Kremlin is likely to have changed this equation somewhat. In the wake of the fumbled putsch, the Russian government moved against Prigozhin's media holdings through steps like the closure of the notorious Internet Research Agency troll farm.[122] The extent of these changes to the scope, reach and resourcing of Russia's disinformation ecosystem, however, likely will not be known for some time.)

By comparison, Western expenditures on countering disinformation and propaganda remain paltry. In the United States, funding for public diplomacy has not risen by any appreciable amount for most of the past two decades.[123] And while Russia's military

121 Interview with NATO strategic communications specialist, Riga, Latvia, February 2023.

122 "Prigozhin-controlled Russian media group shuts after mutiny," Reuters, July 2, 2023, https://www.reuters.com/world/europe/prigozhin-controlled-russian-media-group-shuts-amid-mutiny-fallout-2023-07-02/.

123 The George W. Bush administration's 2003 federal budget allocated some $557 million for the Broadcasting Board of Governors (as the USAGM was then known). When tallied in 2021, the figures remain roughly the same; in its funding request to Congress for Fiscal Year 2022, the USAGM asked for $637.3 million to fund the totality of its operations. See Ilan Berman, "Toward a Public Diplomacy Strategy for the 21st Century," *AFPC Defense Dossier* iss. 31, October 2021, https://www.afpc.org/publications/e-journals/the-future-of-u.s-influence.

aggression against Ukraine in 2022 resulted in a notable acceleration of activities on the part of organs like Radio Free Europe/Radio Liberty, U.S. spending on public diplomacy, though now rising nominally, remains meager by comparison. In its funding request to Congress for 2023, for instance, the United States Agency for Global Media (USAGM) requested $840 million to bankroll the entirety of its outreach.[124] That figure amounts to just over half of the annual information operations budget of Russia alone, to say nothing of China, Iran, and a range of other international actors who are actively attempting to shape global attitudes in an anti-Western and anti-American direction.

Similarly, the budget of the State Department's Global Engagement Center (GEC), the U.S. government's principal coordination arm for global counter-disinformation efforts, remains miniscule. In its 2023 request to Congress, the Department of State requested a total of $12 million for the continued operations of the GEC,

---

124 U.S. Agency for Global Media, *FY2023 Congressional Budget Justification*, March 2022, https://www.usagm.gov/wp-content/uploads/2022/03/USAGMBudget_FY23_CBJ_03-25-22-FINAL.pdf.

the same sum as allocated the year prior.[125] In other words, the U.S. government at the moment is simply not signaling to Congress that it sees the counter-disinformation mission as an urgent one requiring serious, sustained investment. It will need to do so if it hopes to make this enterprise both long-lasting and impactful.

ENCOURAGING INDEPENDENT INVESTMENTS IN COUNTER-DISINFORMATION

In assorted Western nations, there is now serious attention being given to the establishment (or expansion) of institutions dedicated to countering Russian disinformation, promoting alternative media, and expanding civic resilience to Russian malign influence. The Hybrid Threats Center of the Czech Republic's Ministry of Interior and the Swedish Defence Ministry's Psychological Defence Agency represent two prominent examples in this regard. In many ways, however, this ecosystem – though vibrant – remains artificial in nature. A consistent complaint heard across a range

---

125 United States Department of State, *Congressional Budget Justification – Department of State, Foreign Operations, and Related Programs,* n.d., https://www.state.gov/wp-content/uploads/2022/06/FY-2023-Congressional-Budget-Justification_Final_508comp.pdf

of European capitals involves a chronic deficit of resources and manpower to fully animate their respective counter-disinformation missions.

While some of this can doubtless be chalked up to typical bureaucratic jockeying for resources, it nonetheless reflects a larger – and potentially serious – problem. To a notable extent, the international counter-disinformation effort currently lacks a steady, reliable stream of dedicated resources. Rather, today's activities across the Western counter-disinformation "enterprise" are bankrolled largely by American funds, with the State Department's Global Engagement Center serving as a major grantor.

This approach makes sense in the near term, creating compatible organizations and international bodies with whom the United States can interface over a shared threat. Over the longer term, however, reliance on U.S. funding risks the creation of a brittle ecosystem, one whose work could be fundamentally disrupted if there is a slowdown or cessation of American funds. Indeed, multiple European officials relayed concerns that their respective governments do not currently allocate sufficient funding to enable ongoing, effective work against Russian information warfare.[126]

---

126 Author's conversations with government and private sector experts in Latvia, Estonia and Lithuania, February 2023.

Here, U.S. politics should be an important consideration. In what amounts to a reflection of the current, fractious state of national discourse, the issue of disinformation has become a political football of sorts within the United States. Among conservatives, suspicions have abounded that, rather than being an impartial endeavor, disinformation has been harnessed by the sitting Biden administration to police discourse on the political Right – fears that were fanned by the personalities associated with, and purported mission of, the Department of Homeland Security's short-lived "Disinformation Governance Board."[127] More recently, such suspicions have been bolstered by credible evidence that a number of actors in the burgeoning counter-disinformation space have either manipulated the issue to arrogate political power to themselves,[128] or weaponized it to stifle outright opposing political speech with which they happen to disagree.[129]

---

127 See, for instance, Monika Richter, "Is Biden's Disinfo Czar Qualified?" *The Bulwark*, May 6, 2022, https://www. thebulwark.com/is-bidens-disinfo-czar-qualified/.

128 Jacob Seigel, "A Guide to Understanding the Hoax of the Century," *Tablet*, March 29, 2023, https://www.tabletmag. com/sections/news/articles/guide-understanding-hoax-century-thirteen-ways-looking-disinformation.

129 Gabe Kaminsky, "Disinformation Inc: Conservative blacklister cited in brief over Biden 'censorship' lawsuit," *Washington Examiner*, April 20, 2023, https://www. washingtonexaminer.com/news/global-disinformation-index-blacklist-lawsuit-biden-censorship.

These revelations, in turn, have led many to discount both the importance and the urgency of countering foreign disinformation. It is therefore impossible to rule out the possibility that a future change in administration in Washington might be accompanied by a dramatic reduction of support for, and funding of, efforts to counter foreign disinformation, with potentially catastrophic downstream consequences for allied governments that currently rely on American aid for their continued functioning in this space.

To prevent such a possibility, the United States needs to encourage its partners in the common struggle against Russian disinformation to allocate sufficient resources of their own to fully fund robust counter-disinformation efforts on an ongoing basis, irrespective of the vagaries of American politics. In much the same way as "burden-sharing" has become a priority in Washington's conversations with its NATO partners about the future of the Alliance, the sustainability of transnational efforts to combat Russian information manipulation depends on a well-resourced multi-nation effort to confront the threat.

NURTURING RUSSIAN EXILE MEDIA

Among the most consequential side-effects of Russia's current military aggression against Ukraine has been a dramatic tightening of its already-unfree media environment. For years, Russian journalists and commentators had suffered through a tightening web of restrictions on their work, as the government of Vladimir Putin made controlling the objective reality of ordinary Russians a major priority.[130] Even so, the advent of the Ukraine war has been accompanied by extensive new constraints on acceptable speech within Russia, to the point that any coverage at variance with the Kremlin's official narrative of the conflict as a "special operation" to liberate the Ukrainian people is now punishable by extensive prison terms.[131] Additionally, a number of opposition outlets (including *Meduza*, *iStories*, and *The Insider*) have been blacklisted as "undesirable organizations" under Russian law, making support of their activities, or collaboration with them,

---

130 For an in-depth examination of the Putin government's manipulation of contemporary Russian media, see Peter Pomerantsev, *Nothing is True and Everything is Possible: The Surreal Heart of the New Russia* (PublicAffairs, 2015).

131 Matt Mathers, "Russian Duma passes law giving 15-year prison sentences for spreading 'false information' about military," *The Independent*, March 4, 2022, https://www.independent.co.uk/news/world/europe/ukraine-war-latest-russia-law-b2028440.html.

tantamount to treason.[132] The aggregate result of these measures has been an exodus of independent and opposition media actors from Russia, and the formation of a new opposition media ecosystem in the West.

The Latvian capital of Riga has emerged as the epicenter of this emerging media sphere, and the home base for much of Russia's transplanted media outlets. Roughly half of the estimated 500 Russian journalists that have relocated to Europe are now based there,[133] and the city has become a key hub for multiple Russian opposition media outlets, including well-known ones such as *Meduza*, *The Insider* and *Novaya Gazeta Europe*, as well as smaller "startup" publications such as *New Tab* and *People of Baikal.*

Supporting Russia's media exiles, and strengthening their ability to tell a qualitatively different story about their home country, represents a strategic interest for the United States and its Western allies. If nurtured correctly, these media outlets have the potential to emerge as potent counterweights

---

132 "Blacklisted: Russia has declared 12 organizations 'undesirable' so far this year. Here's what you need to know about their work," *Meduza*, August 4, 2022, https://meduza.io/en/feature/2022/08/04/blacklisted

133 Author's conversations with Russian exile journalists, Riga, Latvia, February 2023.

to Kremlin propaganda among those Russians who are seeking authentic Russian voices (rather than Western ones) to inform them about the true state of affairs relating to Ukraine and the wider world. Over time, such alternative narratives can play an important role in combatting the propaganda propounded by the Kremlin among the most important target of its messaging: the Russian people themselves. In order for it to be effective, however, significant work needs to be done in at least two discrete areas.

The first is funding. Many Russian opposition media outlets currently operate on shoestring budgets, and their ongoing solvency is uncertain. To date, aid for such publications and outlets has come overwhelmingly from official governmental sources – either those of the U.S. government, channeled through entities like the National Endowment for Democracy (NED), or official European support routed through the Riga-based Baltic Center for Media Excellence and other outlets.[134] This state of affairs has led to a scramble for scarce resources

---

134 A comparatively recent, and extremely salutary, development in this space has been the National Endowment for Democracy's creation of a dedicated fund allowing private sector donors to likewise assist Russian opposition media outlets. However, it is not clear as of this writing what the long-term impact of this innovation will be – and whether significant funds for Russian opposition media will be raised via this channel.

among Russian media outlets, as well as a competitive environment in which, by necessity, smaller publications are forced to provide their content to their larger rivals, something which could lead to them being subsumed over time. A revamped strategy of financial support for Russian opposition media, one geared specifically toward nurturing smaller, more vulnerable media sources operating in this space, could greatly aid the durability and vibrancy of the emerging Russian opposition media sphere.

Additionally, at least some professionalization of this cohort is needed. While many Russian journalists operate at the highest standards of the profession, not all do. Because of their strong anti-war and anti-Kremlin sentiments, some are more akin to "opinion journalists or activists" than to objective journalists in the Western sense of the word.[135] As a result, there is a need for "professionalization" courses and institutions to help these reporters adapt their skills and focus to life and work outside of Russia. To this end, the United States should encourage closer collaboration with – and training of – Russian exile journalists, with Radio

---

135 Author's conversations with European Union officials in Brussels, Belgium, October 2022.

Free Europe/Radio Liberty's recently established bureau in Riga, Latvia serving as a logical hub for such work.

CONCLUSION: SEEING RUSSIAN DISINFORMATION IN GEOPOLITICAL CONTEXT

As the foregoing makes clear, Russian disinformation and the larger phenomenon of Russian-driven information disorder represent a significant – and enduring – challenge to American interests. This is so not only because of the Kremlin's long-running, and exceedingly well-resourced, effort to destabilize pluralistic societies threatens the Western democratic order. It is also the case because Russia's expertise in information warfare is increasingly being put to use by other like-minded regimes to advance their own geopolitical goals and objectives.

The past several years have provided ample evidence of such collaboration, which experts have termed "authoritarian learning." At the height of the coronavirus pandemic, for instance, the European Union's European External Action Service (EEAS) assessed that false Russian disinformation about COVID-19 was being taken up and amplified by both China and Iran in what amounted to a "trilateral convergence of disinformation narratives" aimed at sowing confusion and diminishing trust in the West among global audiences.[136] So extensive was this collaboration that some authors termed it an "axis of disinformation."[137] More recently, false Russian narratives about Ukraine, formulated in support of the Kremlin's "special military operation" against Kyiv, have been taken up and disseminated

---

136 Rikard Jozwiak, "EU Monitors See Coordinated COVID-19 Disinformation Effort By Iran, Russia, China," Radio Free Europe/Radio Liberty, April 22, 2020, https://www.rferl.org/a/eu-monitors-sees-coordinated-covid-19-disinformation-effort-by-iran-russia-china/30570938.html.

137 Andrew Whiskeyman and Michael Berger, "Axis of Disinformation: Propaganda from Iran, Russia, and China on COVID-19," Washington Institute Fikra Forum *Policy Analysis*, February 2021, https://www.washingtoninstitute.org/policy-analysis/axis-disinformation-propaganda-iran-russia-and-china-covid-19.

by China as part of the so-called "no limits" partnership between Russia and the PRC.[138]

These developments highlight an ominous convergence, whereby Russia's expertise in manipulating the information space has begun to enhance the respective disinformation enterprises of like-minded authoritarian regimes. As a result, the United States and its partners in the West will face a more sophisticated, multifaceted, and hostile informational environment in the years ahead.

All of which makes upgrading the Western response to Russian disinformation essential. Given the commonalities in techniques and narratives now visible between the Kremlin and its ideological fellow-travelers, effectively identifying, countering, and neutralizing Russian disinformation will invariably aid the U.S. in dealing with the informational challenges posed by other malign actors as well.

Countering Russian disinformation is likewise central to America's unfolding "great power competition" with China. In recent years, the United States has steadily gravitated away from

---

138 See, for instance, David Bandurski, "China and Russia are joining forces to spread disinformation," Brookings Institution, March 11, 2022, https://www.brookings.edu/techstream/china-and-russia-are-joining-forces-to-spread-disinformation/.

the long-held notion that expanded trade ties and commercial activity would, over time, make Beijing a "responsible stakeholder" on the world stage. Instead, successive administrations have embraced a more sober reading of China's global ambitions under the leadership of Xi Jinping, and the need for long-term strategic competition with it.

By necessity, this contest will take place, at least in part, in the ideological domain. Over the past several years, as part of its efforts to revise the global order in its favor, China has promoted a distinct alternative model of development, governance and norms. This effort is both more ambitious and more far-reaching than Moscow's manipulation of the information space, which is confined to utilizing a "firehose of falsehood" to obscure objective reality and shape perceptions in its favor.[139] By contrast, Beijing seeks a more sweeping goal: to promote an alternative to the Western liberal order in which states are forced to make a clear trade-off between prosperity and personal freedoms.[140] Moreover,

---

139 Paul and Matthews, "The Russian 'Firehose of Falsehood' Propaganda Model: Why It Might Work and Options to Counter It."

140 See, for instance, Sean Golden, "China's "enlightened authoritarianism' as an alternative to liberal democracy," CIDOB *Opinion*, March 2022, https://www.cidob.org/en/ publications/publication_series/opinion/2022/china_s_ enlightened_authoritarianism_as_an_alternative_to_ liberal_democracy.

Beijing is making concrete progress in a number of world regions, with Chinese information manipulation shaping continental attitudes and distorting regional media markets around the world.[141]

The stakes in this informational contest are exceedingly high. In the West, attitudes toward the PRC have soured appreciably in recent years as a result of a variety of factors, ranging from the aggressive "wolf warrior diplomacy" of its diplomats to the country's increasingly assertive, expeditionary foreign policy under the guidance of Chinese president Xi Jinping.[142] In the "Global South," however, China's "discourse power" is considerably stronger – with Beijing's investments and its ideological messaging succeeding in shaping regional perceptions in places like Africa and the Middle

---

141 See, for instance, Joshua Kurlantzick, *Beijing's Global Media Offensive: China's Uneven Campaign to Influence Asia and the World* (Oxford University Press, 2022).

142 Laura Silver, Christine Huang and Laura Clancy, "China's Approach to Foreign Policy Gets Largely Negative Reviews in 24-Country Survey," Pew Research Center, July 27, 2023, https://www.pewresearch.org/global/2023/07/27/chinas-approach-to-foreign-policy-gets-largely-negative-reviews-in-24-country-survey/.

East in a more pro-Chinese direction.[143] As a consequence, a real global divide is emerging in terms of public opinion toward the PRC, one which will help shape the course of strategic competition between Washington and Beijing.

This, in turn, elevates the urgency of the United States adopting a real, sustainable response to Russian disinformation. For, if Washington fails to properly address the more limited challenge posed by Russia's manipulation of the information space, it will have little hope of countering the comprehensive alternative worldview now being proffered by China, with dire consequences for America's global standing in the decades ahead.

143 Michael Robbins, "Public Views of U.S.-China Competition in MENA," Princeton University, July 2022, https://www.arabbarometer.org/wp-content/uploads/ABVII_US-China_Report-EN-1.pdf; Carlos Mureithi, "Africans' favorable view of China comes with one small caveat," *Quartz*, November 17, 2021, https://qz.com/africa/2090221/africans-favorable-view-of-china-comes-with-one-small-caveat; Ivor Ichikowitz and Aloysius Uche Ordu, "African Youth Survey reveals sustained optimism and shifting priorities," Brookings Institution, July 20, 2022, https://www.brookings.edu/articles/african-youth-survey-reveals-sustained-optimism-and-shifting-priorities/.

ABOUT THE AUTHOR

ILAN BERMAN is Senior Vice President of the
American Foreign Policy Council in Washington,
DC. An expert on regional security in the Middle
East, Central Asia, and the Russian Federation,
he has consulted for the U.S. Central Intelligence
Agency as well as the U.S. Departments of State
and Defense, and has also provided assistance on

foreign policy and national security issues to a range of governmental agencies and congressional offices. He has been called one of America's "leading experts on the Middle East and Iran" by CNN.

Mr. Berman is a member of the Associated Faculty at Missouri State University's Department of Defense and Strategic Studies. A frequent writer and commentator, he has written for the *Wall Street Journal, Foreign Affairs*, the *New York Times, Foreign Policy*, the *Washington Post* and *USA Today*, among many other publications.

Mr. Berman is the editor of six books: *Dismantling Tyranny: Transitioning Beyond Totalitarian Regimes* (Rowman & Littlefield, 2005), co-edited with J. Michael Waller; *Taking on Tehran: Strategies for Confronting the Islamic Republic* (Rowman & Littlefield, 2007); *Iran's Strategic Penetration of Latin America* (Lexington Books, 2015), co-edited with Joseph Humire; *The Logic of Irregular War: Asymmetry and America's Adversaries* (Rowman & Littlefield, 2017); *Digital Dictators: Media, Authoritarianism, and America's New Challenge* (Rowman & Littlefield, 2018); and, most recently, *Wars of Ideas: Theology, Interpretation and Power in the Muslim World* (Rowman & Littlefield, 2021).

He is also the author of five others: *Tehran Rising: Iran's Challenge to the United States* (Rowman & Littlefield, 2005), *Winning the Long War: Retaking the Offensive Against Radical Islam* (Rowman & Littlefield, 2009), *Implosion: The End of Russia and What It Means for America* (Regnery Publishing, 2013); *Iran's Deadly Ambition: The Islamic Republic's Quest for Global Power* (Encounter Books, 2015), and *The Fight for Iran: Opposition Politics, Protest, and the Struggle for the Soul of a Nation* (Rowman & Littlefield, 2020).

www.ingramcontent.com/pod-product-compliance
Lightning Source LLC
Chambersburg PA
CBHW032355280326
41935CB00008B/577